LAND'S END

ABOUT a fourth part of the matter contained in this volume has appeared in the *Saturday Review* and the *Speaker*, and I am obliged to the editors of those journals for their permission to use it here.

LAND'S END
A Naturalist's Impressions in West Cornwall

W.H. HUDSON

NONSUCH

First published 1908
Copyright © in this edition 2005
Nonsuch Publishing Ltd

Nonsuch Publishing Limited
The Mill, Brimscombe Port, Stroud, Gloucestershire, GL5 2QG
www.nonsuch-publishing.com

British Library Cataloguing in Publication Data.
A catalogue record for this book is available from the British Library.

ISBN 1-84588-029-3

Typesetting and origination by Nonsuch Publishing Limited
Printed in Great Britain by Oaklands Book Services Limited

CONTENTS

Introduction to the Modern Edition   7

1.   Wintering in West Cornwall   9
2.   Gulls at St. Ives   19
3.   Cornwall's Connemara   25
4.   Old Cornish Hedges   31
5.   Bolerium: the End of All the Land   37
6.   Castles by the Sea   45
7.   The British Pelican   51
8.   Bird Life in Winter   59
9.   The People and the Farms   67
10.   An Impresson of Penzance   79
11.   Manners and Morals   87
12.   Cornish Humour   97
13.   The Poetic Spirit   111
14.   Winter Aspects and a Bird Visitation   125
15.   A Great Frost   135
16.   A Native Naturalist   145
17.   The Coming of Spring   157
18.   Some Early Flowers   165
19.   The Furze in its Glory   175
20.   Pilgrims at the Land's End   181

Index   189

INTRODUCTION TO THE MODERN EDITION

AT the western extremity of Cornwall lies Land's End, a windswept and wave-battered peninsular where the island of Britain meets the Atlantic Ocean. This book, however, is not just about the place where the land runs out: it is about the whole of western Cornwall, its landscape, natural history and people. Cornwall holds a special position within Britain: although administratively an English county, the Cornish have their own distinctive identity as a Celtic people, with their own flag, patron saint and language. *Land's End* is an account of the visits paid by the naturalist W.H. Hudson to the land west of the River Tamar.

Hudson's travels take him around the spur of land which juts out into the Atlantic at the extreme west of Cornwall. He visits both St Ives and Penzance, but devotes most of his time to the more rural areas, such as the stretch of coastline between St Ives and Land's End, and Land's End itself. St Ives is an enchanting place, a rabbit-warren of houses and cottages around the harbour from where a fleet of one hundred and fifty fishing boats sailed. Penzance, though, was a far more bustling place, especially on market days, full of people and animals. It is Land's End, however, described by Humphrey Davey as 'dark Bolerium, seat of storms', that takes the greatest hold on Hudson's imagination. Despite its rocky and windswept loneliness, he found 'the end of all the land' invested 'with a sublimity and fascination not its own.'

As a naturalist, Hudson's primary concern is with the wildlife of Cornwall and in particular the birds that he observed there. As a comparatively narrow area of land with a long coastline, there were many seabirds in evidence, of which gulls predominated. Rivalling the gulls for the fish to be found in Cornish waters were the gannets, the 'British pelicans.' While the gulls and the gannets were not regarded with any particular hostility by the fishermen, ravens were another story: the religious and the superstitious would shout abuse at the birds and even try to destroy their nests. He was shocked at the attitude of the Cornish towards small birds, who would catch them with baited hooks, apparently for sport.

About the nature of the Cornish, Hudson is particularly forthright. He recorded his observations and thoughts about the people as he did wildlife and was of the opinion, as were the Cornish themselves, that they were a race apart from the rest of Britain: Cornish, not English. Hudson found them very difficult to understand, although when he visited in the early twentieth century, the Cornish language was effectively at its nadir (the last monoglot Cornish-speaker had died in 1777) and there were very few who spoke it. When a Cornish farmer explained the local political sitution to him, he was interested less in what he said than the way in which he said it. He identified a Cornish sense of humour which was different to that of the rest of Britain, as well as other characteristics of 'manners and morals.'

Hudson's description of west Cornwall and the people who lived there provides a fascinating insight into a corner of Britain often neglected or simply assumed to be a part of England. The people of Cornwall had then and still have a sense of their own identity, something that goes deeper than just having their own flag. Hudson conveys this individuality with the skill of an experienced naturalist, as well as providing details of the landscape and wildlife of this beautiful place where Britain ends.

William Henry Hudson was born in 1841 in Argentina and his childhood and youth were spent on his father's *estancia* on the Argentinian *pampas*. He made many excursions into remote areas, which provided ample material for books such as *Argentine Ornithology* (1888-89), *The Naturalist in La Plata* (1892) and *Idle Days in Patagonia* (1893). He moved to England in 1869, marrying Emily Wingrave, a woman fifteen years older than himself, in 1876. They kept boarding-houses in order to make a living and it was not until the publication of *The Naturalist in La Plata* in 1892 that he made a name for himself. Still financially unsuccessful, a Civil List pension of £150 *per annum* was awarded to him in 1901 which allowed him to travel to research books such as *Land's End*. The novel *Green Mansions* (1904), a romance set in South America, achieved great popularity. In all, his collected works, published in 1923, fill twenty-five volumes. He died England in 1922. Two species of South American bird are named after him and there is a sculpture by Jacob Epstein in Hyde Park which is dedicated to his memory.

WINTERING IN WEST CORNWALL

"KNOW," said wise old Fuller, "most of the rooms of thy native country before thou goest over the threshold thereof. Especially England presents thee with so many observables." But if we were to follow this advice there would be no getting out of the country at all. It is too rich in its way: the rooms are too many and too well-furnished with observables. Take my case. I have been going on rambles about the land for a good many years, and though the West Country had greatest attraction for me, I never got over the Tamar, nor even so far as Plymouth, simply because I had not the time, albeit my time was my own. Or because there was enough and more than enough to satisfy me on this side of the boundary. It is true one desires to see and know all places, but is in no hurry to go from a rich to a poor one. I was told by every one of my friends that it was the most interesting county in England, and doubtless it is so to them, but I knew it could not be so to me because of the comparative poverty of the fauna, seeing that the observables which chiefly draw me are the living creatures—the wild life and not hills and valleys and granite and serpentine cliffs and seas of Mediterranean blue. These are but the setting of the shining living gems, and we know the finest of these, which gave most lustre to the scene, have been taken out and cast away.

Cornwall to me was just the Land's End—"dark Bolerium, seat of storms"—that famous foreland of which a vast but misty picture formed in childhood remains in the mind, and if I ever felt any strong desire to visit Cornwall it was to look upon that scene. Then came a day in November 1905, when, having settled to go away somewhere for a season, I all at once made up my mind to visit the unknown peninsula and to go straight away to the very end. It almost astonished me when I alighted from my train at St. Ives to think I had travelled three hundred and twenty odd miles with less discomfort and weariness than I usually experience on any journey of a hundred. It is common, I think, for lovers of walking to dislike the railway. So smoothly had I been carried in this flight to the furthest west that I might have been sailing in a balloon; and as for the time occupied, it would surely be no bad progress for a migrating bird, travelling, let us say, from Middlesex to Africa, to cover the distance I had come in a little more than seven hours!

St. Ives is on the north side of the rounded western extremity of Cornwall, and from the little green hill, called the "Island," which rises above and partly shelters the town, you look out upon the wide Atlantic, the sea that has always a trouble on it and that cannot be quiet; and standing there with the great waves breaking on the black granite rocks at your feet, they will tell you that there is no land between you and America. Nevertheless, after London, I wanted no better climate; for though it rained heavily on many days in December and the wind blew with tremendous force, the temperature was singularly mild, with an agreeable softness in the air and sunshine breaking out on the cloudiest days. The weather could be described as "delicate" with tempestuous intervals. On bright, windless days I saw the peacock butterfly abroad and heard that idle song of the corn bunting, associated in our minds with green or yellow fields and sultry weather. I was still more surprised one day late in December at meeting with a lively wheatear, flitting from stone to stone near the Land's End. This one had discovered that it was not necessary to fly all the way to North Africa to find a place to winter in. Early in February I found the adder abroad.

The town, viewed from the outside—the old fishing town, which does not include the numerous terraces and other modern erections on the neighbouring heights—appears very small indeed. It is small, for when you once master its intricacies you can walk through from end to end in about five or six minutes. But the houses are closely packed, or rather jumbled together with the narrowest and crookedest streets and courts in which to get about or up and down. They have a look of individuality, like a crowd of big rough men pushing and elbowing one another for room, and you can see how this haphazard condition has come about when you stumble by chance on a huge mass of rock thrusting up out of the earth among the houses. There was, in fact, just this little sheltered depression in a stony place to build upon, and the first settlers, no doubt, set their houses just where and how they could among the rocks, and when more room was wanted more rocks were broken down and other houses added until the town as we find it resulted. It is all rude and irregular, as if produced by chance or nature, and altogether reminds one of a rabbit warren or the interior of an ants' nest.

It cannot be nice to live in such a warren or rookery, except to those who were born in it; nevertheless it is curiously attractive, and I, although a disliker of towns or congeries of houses, found a novel pleasure in poking about it, getting into doorways and chance openings to be out of the way of a passing cart which as a rule would take up the whole width of the street. Outside the houses hung the wet oilskins and big sea-boots to dry, and at the doors women with shawls over their heads stand gossiping. When the men are asleep or away and the children at school these appear to be the only inhabitants, except the cats. You find one at every few yards usually occupied with the head of a mackerel or herring. The appearance was perhaps even better by night, when the narrow crooked ways are very dark except at some rare spot where a lamp casts a mysterious light on some quaint old corner building and affords a glimpse into a dimly-seen street beyond ending in deep gloom.

In this nest or hive are packed about eight hundred fishermen with their wives and children, their old fathers and mothers, and other members of the community who do not go in the boats. The fishermen are the most interesting in appearance; it is a relief, a positive pleasure, to see in England a people clothed not in that ugly dress which is now so universal, but in one suitable to their own life and work—their ponderous sea-boots and short shirt-shaped oilies of many shades of colour from dirty white and pale yellow to deep reds and maroons. In speech and manners they are rough and brusque, and this, too, like their dress and lurching gait, comes, as it were, by nature; for of all occupations, this of wresting a poor and precarious livelihood from the wind-vexed seas under the black night skies in their open boats is assuredly the hardest and most trying to a man's temper. The navvy and the quarryman, the labourer on the land, here where the land is half rock, even the tin-miner deep down in the bowels of the earth, have a less discomfortable and anxious life. That they are not satisfied with it one soon discovers; Canada calls them, and Africa, and other distant lands, and unhappily, as in most places, it is always the best men that go. Possibly this accounts for the change for the worse in the people which some have noted in recent years. Nevertheless they are a good people still, righteous in their own peculiar way, and so independent that in bad times, as when the fishing fails, hunger and cold are more endurable to them than charity. They are a clannish people, and it is consequently not to be wondered at that they have no subscription clubs or friendly societies of any kind to aid them in times of want and sickness such as are now almost universal among the working classes. These benefits of our civilisation will doubtless come to them in time: then their clannishness—the old "One and All" spirit of Cornishmen generally—being no longer needed, will decay. It is after all but another word for solidarity, the strong, natural, or family bond which unites the members of a community which was once, in ruder ages, everywhere, to make social life possible, and has survived here solely because of Cornwall's isolated position. Unfortunately we cannot make any advance, cannot gain anything anywhere, without a corresponding loss somewhere. Will it be better for this people when the change comes—when the machine we call "civilisation" has taken the place of the spirit of mutual help in the members of the community? 'Tis an idle question, since we cannot have two systems of life. At present, in our "backward" districts, we have two, but they are in perpetual conflict, and one must overcome the other; and if there be any beautiful growths in the old and unfit, which is passing away, they must undoubtedly perish with it.

One of the most pleasing traits of the Cornish people, which is but one manifestation of the spirit I have been speaking about, is their love for little children. Nowhere in the kingdom, town or country, do you see a brighter, happier, better-dressed company of small children than here in the narrow stony ways of the old fishing town. The rudest men exhibit a strange tenderness towards their little ones; and not only their own, since they regard all children with a kind of parental feeling. An incident which occurred in the early part of December, and its effects on the people, may be given here as an illustration. One morning when the boats came in it was reported that one of the men had been lost. "Poor fellow!" was all that was said about it. And that is how it is all the world over among men who have dangerous occupations: the loss of a comrade is a not uncommon experience, and the shock is very slight and quickly vanishes. But there was no such indifference when, two or three days later, one of the herring-boats brought in the corpse of a small child which had been fished up in the Bay—a pretty little well-nourished boy, decently dressed, aged about two years and a half. Where the child belonged and how it came to be in the sea was not discovered until long afterwards, but the intensity of the feeling displayed was a surprise to me. For several days little else was talked of both in St. Ives and the villages and farms in the neighbourhood, and they talked of it, both men and women, with tears in their voices as though the death of this unknown child had been a personal loss.

This incident served to recall others, of St. Ives children lost and drowned in past years, especially this very pathetic one of three little things who went out to pick flowers one afternoon and were lost. They were two sisters, aged eight and nine respectively, and their little brother, about six or seven years old. They rambled along the rough heath by Carbis Bay to the Towans, near Lelant, where, climbing about among the sand-hills, they lost all sense of direction. There meeting a man who spoke roughly to them and ordered them home they became terrified and ran away to the sea-front, and, climbing down the cliff, hid themselves in a cave they found there. By-and-by it began to grow dark, and there were sounds above as of loud talking and shouts and of a galloping horse, all which added to their fear and caused them to go further into their dark wet house of refuge. They did not know, poor children, that the cries were uttered by those who were seeking for them! After dark the tide rose and covered the sandy floor of the cave, and to escape it they climbed on to a rocky shelf where they could keep dry, and there huddled together to keep warm, and being very tired, they eventually fell asleep. In the morning when it grew light the sisters woke, stiff and cold, to find that their poor little brother had fallen from the ledge in his sleep and had been carried out by the sea. His body was recovered later. The two survivors, now middle-aged women, still live in the town.

The most interesting hour of the day at St. Ives was in the afternoon or evening, the time depending on the tide, when the men issued from their houses and came lurching down the little crooked stone streets and courts to the cove or harbour to get the boats out for the night's fishing. It is a very small harbour in the corner of the bay—a roughly shaped half-moon with two little stone piers for horns, with just room enough inside to accommodate the fleet of about one hundred and fifty boats. The best spectacle is when they are taken out at or near sunset in fair weather, when the subdued light gives a touch of tenderness and mystery to sea and sky, and the boats, singly, in twos and threes, and in groups of half a dozen, drift out from the harbour and go away in a kind of procession over the sea. The black forms on the moving darkening water and the shapely deep-red sails glowing in the level light have then a beauty, an expression, which comes as a surprise to one unaccustomed to such a scene. The expression is due to association—to vague suggestions of a resemblance in this to other scenes. We may be unable to recall them; the feeling returns but with the mental image of the scene which originally produced it. It was not until I had watched the boats going out on two or three successive evenings that an ancient memory returned to me.

Sitting or walking by the margin of some wide lake or marsh in a distant land, I am watching a company of birds of some large majestic kind—stork, wood-ibis, or flamingo—standing at rest in the shallow water, which reflects their forms. By-and-by one of the birds steps out of the crowd and moves leisurely away, then, slowly unfolding his broad wings, launches himself on the air and goes off, flying very low over the water. Another follows, then, after an interval, another, then still others, in twos and threes and half-dozens, until the last bird has opened his wings and the entire flock is seen moving away in a loose procession over the lake.

Just in that way did the crowd of boats move by degrees from their resting-place, shake out their wing-like sails, and stream away over the sea.

That was one scene; there were faint suggestions of many others, only a few of which I could recover; one was of large, dark red-winged butterflies, seen at rest with closed wings, congregated on wind-swayed reeds and other slender plants. It was the shape and deep red colour of the sails and the way they hung from the masts and cordage which restored this butterfly picture to my mind. And in every instance in which a resemblance could be traced it turned out to be to some natural and invariably to a beautiful object or scene. The spectacle had, in fact, that charm, which is so rare in man's work, of something wholly natural, which fits into the scene and is part and parcel with nature itself.

In buildings we get a similar effect at the two extremes—in the humblest and the highest work of man's hands; in the small old thatched and rose- and creeper-covered cottage in perfect harmony with its surroundings, and in ancient majestic castles and cathedrals, in which the sharp lines and contours have been blurred by decay of the material and the whole surface weathered and stained with lichen and alga and in many cases partially draped with ivy.

It struck me before I had been long in St. Ives that, in spite of the delightful mildness of the climate and the charm of the place, nobody but myself was wintering there. The lodging-houses were quite empty; the people were the natives or else the artists, who form a pretty numerous colony. The few others to be seen were visitors for the day from Penzance, Falmouth, or some other spot in the "Cornish Riviera." This was not a cause of regret, seeing there were birds for society, especially that old favourite, the jackdaw. Doubtless he is to be seen there all the year round as he is so common a town bird all over the country, but at St. Ives many of the cliff-breeding daws settle down regularly for the winter and exist very comfortably on the fish and other refuse thrown into the streets. Very soon I established a sort of friendship with a few of these birds; for birds I must have, in town or country—free birds I mean, as the captive bird only makes me melancholy—and in winter I feed them whether they are in want or not. It is an old habit of mine, first practised in early life in June and July, the cold winter months in the southern hemisphere, in a land where the English sparrow was not. Now, unhappily, he is there and a great deal too abundant. I fed a better sparrow in those vanished days, smaller and more prettily shaped than our bird, with a small crest on his head and a sweet delicate little song. But in England one really gets far more pleasure from feeding the birds on account of the number of different species which are willing to be our pensioners. At St. Ives I first stayed at a house in The Terrace facing the sea-front, and there were no gardens there, so that I had to feed them out in the road. First there were only sparrows, then a pair of jackdaws turned up, and soon others joined them until I had about a score of them. By-and-by a very big shaggy sheep-dog, belonging to a carter, discovered that there was food to be got at eight o'clock at that spot in the road, and he too came very punctually every day and thoughtlessly gobbled it all up himself. After two or three days of this sort of thing, I felt that it ought not to be allowed to continue, and as the daws were of the same mind and loyally seconded my efforts to stop it, we were soon successful. My plan was to go out and scatter the scraps and crusts far and wide over the road, and while the greedy dog galloped about from crust to crust the daws, hovering overhead, dropped down and snatched them one by one away before he could reach them.

Later, when leaving St. Ives, I asked the landlady to explain to the birds on the following morning the reason of there being nothing for them, and to request them to go quietly away. They were very intelligent, I said, and would understand; but on my return, a month later, she said they had not understood the message, or had not believed her, as they had continued to come for several mornings, and had seemed very much put out. It was plain they had kept an eye on that house during my absence, for on going out with scraps on the morning after my return they promptly reappeared in full force on the scene.

There are few persons to feed the birds in those parts, and those few, I fancy, are mostly visitors from other counties. It amused me to see how the natives regarded my action; the passer-by would stop and examine the scraps or crusts, then stare at me, and finally depart with a puzzled expression on his countenance, or perhaps smiling at the ridiculous thing he had witnessed.

The following winter (1906–7) I found a lodging in another part of the town, in a terrace rather high up, where I could look from my window at the Bay over the tiled roofs of the old town. Here I had a front garden to feed the birds in, and, better still, the entire jackdaw population of St. Ives, living on the roofs as is their custom, were under my eyes comfortably. I discovered that they filled up a good deal of their vacant time each morning in visiting the chimneys from which smoke issued, just to inform themselves, as it seemed, what was being cooked for breakfast. This was their pastime, and watching them was mine. Numbers of daws would be seen, singly, in pairs, and in groups of three or four to half a dozen, sitting on the roofs all over the place. As the morning progressed and more and more chimneys sent out smoke, they would become active visiting the chimneys, where, perching on the rims, they would put their heads down to get the smell, rising from the pot or frying-pan on the fire below. If a bird remained long perched on a chimney-pot, his neighbours would quickly conclude that he had come upon a particularly interesting smell and rush off to share it with him. When the birds were too many there would be a struggle for places, and occasionally it happened that a puff of dense black smoke would drive them all off together.

A dozen incidents of this kind could be witnessed any morning, and I was as much entertained as if I had been observing not birds but a lot of lively, tricky little black men with grey pates inhabiting the roofs. One morning when watching a pair perched facing each other on a chimney-top, their movements and gestures made me imagine that I knew just what they were saying. First one leaning over the rim would thrust his head down into the smoke and keep it there some time, the other would follow suit, then pulling themselves up they would stare at each other for half a minute, then poke their heads down again.

"A funny smell that!" one says. "I can't quite make it out, and yet I seem to know what it is."

"Red herring," suggests the other.

"Nonsense! I know that smell well enough. But I grant you it's just a little like it, only—what shall I say?—this is a thicker sort of smell."

"I'll just have another good sniff," says the second bird. "H'm! I wonder if it's some very old pilchards they've found stowed away in some corner?"

"No," says the first bird, pulling his head out of the smoke and blinking his wicked little grey eyes. "It isn't pilchards. Just one more sniff. I've got it! A very old piece of dry salted conger they're broiling on the coals."

"By Jove, you're right this time! It is a good thick smell! I only wish I could drop down the flue, snatch up that bit of conger, and get clear away with it." "You'd soon have a jolly lot of jacks after you, I fancy. Hullo!

What are those fellows making such a to-do about—down there on that chimney-pot? Let's go and find out."

And away they fly, to drop down and fight for places among the others.

GULLS AT ST. IVES

TO a bird lover the principal charm of St. Ives is in its gull population. Gulls greatly outnumber all the other wild birds of the town and harbour put together, and though they have not the peculiar fascination of the jackdaw, which is due to that bird's intelligence and amusing rascalities, they are very much more beautiful.

Of all feathered creatures gulls are ever the quickest to discover food thrown accidentally in their way by man. In many lands, crows, vultures, carrion hawks, and omnivorous feeders generally acquire the habit of watching the movements of the human hunter and of travellers in desert places for the sake of his leavings. In the gulls this habit is universal; their "wide eyes that search the sea" have discovered that where there is a ship or boat something may be picked up by following it, and in all lands where there is a plough to share the soil the plough is pretty sure to have a following of gulls at his heels. In harbours they are much at home, but are especially attracted to a fishing town, and it would be hard to find one where they make a better appearance than at St. Ives. But not solely on account of their numbers and tameness, since they congregate at all fishing stations and are just as tame and abundant elsewhere. At St. Ives they make a better show because of the picturesque character of the place itself—the small harbour, open to the wide blue bay and the Atlantic, crowded with its forest of tall slim masts resembling a thick grove of larches in winter, while for background there is the little old town, its semicircle of irregular quaint and curious stone-grey and tile-red buildings.

The gulls that congregate here are of several kinds: on most days one can easily count five species, the most abundant being the herring and the lesser black-backed gulls, and with them you generally see one or two great black-backs. Then there are the two small species, the common and the black-headed gull. These, when it comes to a general scramble for the small fishes and other waste, are mere pickers-up of unconsidered trifles on the out skirts of the whirlwind of wings, the real fighting area, and their guttural cries—a familiar sound to Londoners in winter—are drowned in the tempest of hard, piercing, and grinding metallic noises emitted by the bigger birds.

All this noise and fury and scurry of wings of innumerable white forms, mixed up with boats and busy shouting men, comes to be regarded by the people concerned as a necessary part of the whole business, and the bigger the bird crowd and the louder the uproar the better they appear to like it. For their gulls are very dear to them.

One morning when looking on and enjoying the noisy scene, I saw one of the smaller boats left unattended by the men. They had thrown a canvas over the fish, but this the gulls soon succeeded in pulling aside; then those overhead converging poured down in the form of a white column, and the boat was covered from stem to stern with a mass of birds madly fighting for the herrings. The men in other boats close by looked on and laughed; by-and-by they began shouting, but this had no effect, and the struggling and feasting went on until the master of the boat returned and scared them off. He said afterwards that they had devoured half his catch, yet the men who had been standing by looking on had made no real attempt to save the fish.

The gulls know their friends very well; with the man in sea-boots and oilskins they are tamer than any domestic bird; they will take food from his hands and love to settle to rest on the boats and to sit perched like swallows on the mast top. They have not the same confidence towards strangers, and they positively dislike small boys. When boys appear they fly away to a distance. One evening, the men being out of sight, I found three urchins amusing themselves by throwing stones at a few small gulls flying about the sand in search of scraps. "What would you get," I asked them, "if one of the men caught you stoning the gulls?" "Oh!" cried the biggest of the three, drawing his head down between his shoulders in a most expressive way, "we'd get our ears well cuffed." "Very well," I said, "I'm here in their place to-day to look after the birds." In a moment they dropped their stones and taking to their heels vanished in a neighbouring court.

Yet these very boys in a few years' time, when they will be in the boats too, will have the same feeling as the men, and be ready to inflict the severest punishment on any youngster they may catch throwing a pebble at one of their sacred birds!

One day I caught sight of a large ivory-white gull of an unknown species sitting on the water some distance from the shore, and was very anxious to see more of this bird. Two or three days later I was with an artist friend in his studio, and was standing at the window which looks upon a sandy cove at the back of the town. By-and-by a wave of the incoming tide threw up a dead dogfish about three feet long on the white sand within fifty yards of the window. Scarcely was the fish left by the retiring water before a big white-winged gull dropped down upon it—the very bird I had been hoping to encounter again! There it remained, trying to tear a hole in the tough skin, fully five minutes before the returning water took the fish away, so that I had a good chance of examining it through a binocular. It was considerably bigger than the herring gull, with a much more formidable beak and altogether a bolder appearance, and the entire plumage was of a chalky white. It was a glaucous gull—the famous Burgomaster of the Arctic Sea, probably a female in immature plumage. In a few moments other gulls dropped down to get a bite—three herring and one black-backed gull with some smaller gulls—but they were not allowed to taste the fish. When one attempted to come near the white gull looked fixedly at him a couple of moments, then drawing in its head suddenly tipped its beak upwards—an expressive gull gesture corresponding to the snarl of a dog when he is feeding and other dogs approach him. It produced a marked effect on the other gulls; perhaps the Burgomaster, a rare visitor to our seas, was known, from hearsay, to them as a great tyrant.

Talking of this noble stranger to one of the fishermen, I remarked that if a bird collector happened to be about he would certainly have that bird even if compelled to fire into the whole crowd of gulls to kill it. "Then," he returned, "perhaps our men would kill him!"

The curious point is that this feeling should exist and be so strong in a people who have little or no regard for birds generally. The most religious of men, they are at the same time the least humane. The gull, they tell you, is the fisherman's friend; but other sea-birds, which he kills without compunction—the gannet, for instance—are useful to him in the same way as the gull. They also say that the gulls keep the harbour sweet and clean; an explanation probably invented for them by. Some stranger within their gates. The fact is, they cherish an affection for the gulls, though they refuse to confess it, and, being what they are by race, this feeling has acquired the character of a superstition. To injure a gull wilfully is to invite disaster. It may be that the origin of the feeling is simply the fact that gulls gather in vociferous crowds round the boats and in the harbour when the fishing has prospered, and in this way become associated in the fisherman's mind with all those agreeable ideas or images and emotions connected with a good catch—smiles and cheerful words of greeting in the home, with food in abundance, money for the rent and for needed clothes and other good things for the little ones.

On the other hand we may have here a survival of an older superstition, a notion that gulls are in some degree supernatural beings, perhaps drowned mariners and fishermen returned in bird forms to haunt their ancient homes and associate with their human fellow-creatures. The feeling is certainly very strong: I was told that some of the fishermen even in their times of greatest scarcity will always manage at meal-time to put a few crusts and scraps of food into their pockets to throw to the gulls in the harbour.

From all this it might appear that the gulls at St. Ives are having an exceedingly good time, but they are not wholly happy—not happy every day, as they very soon let me know. The fishermen, like the Cornish people generally, are strict Sabbatarians, and from Friday night or Saturday morning, when the boats come in, they do not go out again until the following Monday evening. In a neighbouring fishing village the boats are taken out at the stroke of twelve on Sunday night. The St. Ives men do not like to run it so fine, and the gulls are never able to understand this long break in the fishing. On the Saturday, after feeding, they retire to the sea and the rocks, where they pass the day comfortably enough, sitting with beaks to the wind and digesting a plentiful meal. On Sunday morning they congregate in the harbour with empty stomachs only to find the boats lying empty and idle and all the men away; they do not like it, but they put up with it, and by-and-by loiter off to pick up what they can for themselves, or to wait patiently on the sea and the rocks, through another long twenty-four hours. On Monday morning they are very hungry indeed, and come in with stomachs that scream for food. They come in their thousands, and still nothing for them—the boats lying empty and idle, the men still at home in bed and no movement in the harbour! They cannot and they will not endure it. Then begins a tremendous demonstration of the unemployed. On my first Monday I was roused from slumber before daylight by the uproar It was not now that tempest and tangle of broken, squealing and grinding metallic noises emitted by the big gulls when they are in numbers fighting over their food, it was the loud long wailing call of the bird, incessantly repeated, a thousand wailing like one, and at intervals the dreary laughter-like chorus of short reiterated cries; then again the insistent wailing calls. When it became light they could be seen as a white cloud hanging over the harbour, the birds moving round and round over the idle boats in endless procession, and this went on for about an hour, when, finding that nothing came of it all, they went sadly away.

On yet another morning I was awakened before daylight, but this was a happy occasion, the boats having come in during the small hours laden with the biggest catch of the season. The noise of the birds made me get up and dress in a hurry to go and find out what it was all about. For an hour and a half I stood at the end of the little stone pier watching the cloud and whirlwind of vociferous birds, and should have remained longer but for a singular accident—a little gull tragedy—which brought a sudden end to the feast. The men in fifty boats while occupied in disengaging the fish from the nets were continually throwing the small useless fishes away, and these, falling all round in the water, brought down a perpetual rush and rain of gulls from over head; everywhere they were frantically struggling on the water, while every bird rising with a fish in his beak was instantly swooped down upon and chased by the others. Now one of the excited birds while rushing down by chance struck a rope or spar and fell into the water at the side of a boat, about forty yards from where I was standing. It was a herring gull in mature plumage, and its wing was broken. The bird could not understand this; it made frantic efforts to rise, but the whole force exerted being in one wing merely caused it to spin rapidly round and round. These struggles eventually caused the shattered bone to break through the skin; the blood began to flow and redden the plumage on one side. This was again and again washed off in the succeeding struggles to rise, but every time a pause came the feathers were reddened afresh. At length the poor thing became convinced that It could no longer fly, that it could only swim, and at once ceasing to struggle it swam away from the boats and out towards the open bay. Hardly had it gone a dozen yards from the boat-side where it had fallen before some of the gulls flying near observed it for the first time, and dropping to within three or four yards of the surface hovered over it. Then a strange thing happened. Instantly, as if a shot had been fired to silence them, the uproar in the harbour ceased; the hundreds of gulls fighting on the water rose up simultaneously to join the cloud of birds above, and the whole concourse moved silently away in one direction, forming a dense crowd above the wounded bird. In this formation, suspended at a height of about thirty yards over and moving with him, they travelled slowly out into the middle of the bay.

The silence and stillness in the harbour seemed strange after that tempest of noise and motion, for not a bird had remained behind, nor did one return for at least half an hour; then in small companies they began to straggle back to resume the interrupted feast.

CORNWALL'S CONNEMARA

THE coast country at the end or the western extremity of Cornwall presents an aspect wild and rough as any spot in England. The eighty-miles-long county, which someone compares to a malformed knobbly human leg in shape, narrows down near its termination to a neck or ankle of land no more than six or seven miles wide, with St. Ives Bay on one (the north) side, and Mount's Bay on the other, with its group of places of famous or familiar names—Mousehole, Newlyn, Penzance, Marazion and St. Michael's Mount. Then the land broadens again, forming that rounded bit of country, the westernmost part of England, containing seventy-five or eighty square miles of hilly and moorland country, in great part treeless, with a coastline, from bay to bay, of about thirty miles. Following the coast, one does not wish them more: the most enthusiastic lover of an incult nature, who delights in forcing his way over rocky barriers and through thickets of furze, bogs and rills innumerable, will find these thirty miles as satisfying as any sixty elsewhere. And the roughest, therefore most exhilarating, portion of the coast is that between St. Ives and Land's End, a distance of about twenty miles. This strip of country has been called the Connemara of Cornwall. William Gilpin, that grand old seeker after the picturesque at the end of the eighteenth century, once journeyed into Cornwall, but got no further than Bodmin, as he saw nothing but "a barren and naked country, in all respects as uninteresting as can well be conceived," and he was informed that west of Bodmin it was no better. It is, indeed, worse, and one wonders what, his feelings would have been had he persevered to the very end—to rough "Connemara" and flat, naked Bolerium! His strictures on the scenery would have amused the present generation. For all that repelled Gilpin and those of his time in nature, the barren or "undecorated," as he would say, the harsh and savage and unsuited to human beings, now most attracts us. And of all places inhabited by man this coast country is the most desert-like and desolate in appearance. The black, frowning, wave-beaten cliffs on the one hand, the hills and moors on the other, treeless, strewn abundantly with granite boulders, rough with heath and furze and bracken, the summits crowned with great masses of rock resembling ancient ruined castles. Midway between the hills and the sea, half a mile or so from the cliffs, are the farms, but the small houses and walled fields on the inhabited strip hardly detract from the rude and savage aspect of the country. Nature will be Nature here, and man, like the other inhabitants of the wilderness, has adapted himself to the conditions. The badgers have their earths, the foxes their caverns in the rocks, and the linnet, yellow-hammer, and magpie hide their nests, big and little, in the dense furze bushes: he in like manner builds his dwelling small and low, sheltering as best he can in any slight depression in the ground, or behind thickets of furze and the rocks he piles up. The small naked stone farm-house, with its little out-buildings, corn-stacks, and wood piles huddling round it, seem like a little flock of goats drawn together for company and shelter in some rough desert place on a cold windy day. Looking from a hill-top on one of the small groups of buildings—and in some instances two or three farms have clubbed their houses together for better protection from the blast—they resemble toy houses, and you have the fancy that you could go down and pick them up and put them in your pocket.

The coast road, running from village to village, winding much, now under, now over the hills, comes close to some of the farms and leaves others at a distance; but all these little human centres are united by a footpath across the fields. It is very pleasant to follow this slight track, this connecting thread, which brings to mind Richard Carew's account of the poor Cornish farmers of his time, three centuries ago, when he says that "amongst themselves they agree well and company lovingly together." I recall, too, that some social rodents, that live in communities, in collections of burrows or villages, have a track of that kind leading from village to village, worn by the feet of the little animals in visiting their neighbours. The fields being small you have innumerable stiles to cross in a five or a ten miles' walk; but they do not want climbing, as they are very nearly all of that Cornish type made with half a dozen or more large slabs of granite placed gridiron-wise almost flush with the ground. You step easily over the stones: but the cattle do not follow, since, owing to their inability to see just where their feet will be set, their legs would come down between the slabs.

Cows are in most of the fields, the dairy being the main thing in these farms; and next to the small Jersey-like cow, the native breed, the pig ranks in importance. It is pleasant to see the pigs in these parts, as they are allowed more liberty in the fields and about the house than they usually get in other places; or, indeed, anywhere on this side of St. George's Channel. If not "the gintleman that pays the rint," the pig contributes a good deal towards it, and short of liberty to walk in at the front door and take his place in the family circle he has every consideration paid him. On going up to a farm house one is sometimes obliged to get round or step over a pig lying comfortably in the path. One day, going to call on some friends who had taken lodgings at a small farm, I found a portly sow lying in the way a dozen yards or so from the front door. My friends were getting ready for a walk, and when we came out the sow got up and, placing herself at the side of the lady, set out with us. We all tried our best to turn her back, shouting indignantly at her and pushing her away with our sticks and boots, but all in vain—she would come. "I'm to blame," said the lady. "When we first came we had tea out of doors, and when this pig came up to look at us I foolishly gave her a slice of bread and butter and spoke kindly to her, and now I can't get away from her. I give her nothing, and I try to escape her attention, but she watches the door, and when she sees me with my things on she insists on keeping with me even if I walk miles. It is most inconvenient." It certainly was, and we carefully avoided the village for fear of remarks. Fowls, too, are reared in numbers, and it is a great grievance of the farmers that foxes must be religiously preserved along this coast where they cannot be hunted. Here, again, I am reminded of Carew's *Survey of Cornwall*, in which he writes: "The fox planteth his dwelling in the steep cliffs of the seaside, where he possesseth holds, so many in number, so dangerous of access, and so full of windings, as in a manner it falleth out a matter impossible to disseize him of his ancient inheritance." He still keeps it, and after three centuries is more secure in it than ever, since there is now no stronger law than this unwritten one which gives immunity to the fox.

As a rule, several dogs are kept on the farm; but he cares little for them. His fastness is close by in the cliffs, and between it and the farm there is wilderness of furze bushes and stone fences, the ins and outs of which he knows better than the dogs. They cannot come near him. At one place the farmer's wife told me the foxes came about the house almost every night and started barking, whereupon the dogs barked in reply, and this would go on, bark fox, bark dog, by the hour, keeping them awake, until at last the dogs, tired of the useless contest, would go to sleep; then the foxes would sneak in to see what they could pick up.

There is very little cultivation—hardly more than is required for the use of the farm, and in many fields even this little is carried on under difficulties on account of the stones. The stones are taken out and piled on to the walls or hedges at the side, and though this process has been going on for centuries, many boulders and huge blocks of granite still remain in the little fields. I was amused one day at the sight of a field of only about two acres on which I counted one hundred and thirty-five stones appearing like huge mushrooms and toadstools over the ground. Corn had been grown on it, and I asked the farmer how it was managed. He answered that he would laugh to see a man and horses from any other part of the country try to cultivate that field and others like it. Here the men are used to it, and horses know their part so well that if the share touches a stone they stop instantly and wait for the ploughman's word to move on.

This same farmer told me that one day last summer a lady visitor staying in the neighbourhood came to where he was doing some work and burst out in praise of the place, and told him she envied him his home in the dearest, sweetest, loveliest spot on earth. "That's what you think, ma'am," he returned, "because you're here for a week or two in summer when it's fine and the heath in bloom. Now I think it's the poorest, ugliest, horriblest place in the whole world, because I've got to live in it and get my living out of it."

They certainly have to work hard to make the two pounds per acre they have to pay for their stony fields. But they are a tough, industrious, frugal people, in many instances little removed from peasants in their way of living, and are strongly attached to their rude homes and rough country. If you tell them that their lot is exceedingly hard, that they pay too high a rent, and so on, enumerating all the drawbacks, they assent eagerly, and will put in many little touches to make the picture darker; but if you then advise them to throw up their farms and migrate to some place you can name, in the Midlands say, where they will pay less for better land, and be out of the everlasting wind which tears every green leaf to shreds and makes their lives a perpetual discomfort, they shake their heads. They cannot endure the thought of leaving their homes. It is only the all-but complete ruin of the tin-mining industry that has sent so many Cornishmen into exile in distant lands. But these wanderers are always thinking of home and come back when they can. One meets them every day, young and middle-aged men, back from Africa, Australia, America; not to settle down, since there is nothing for them to do—not just yet at all events; but because they have saved a little and can afford to take that long journey for the joy of seeing the dear old faces again, and the dear familiar land which proved so uninteresting to the reverend author of *Forest Scenery*.

But farming, unlike the mining and fishing industries, cannot fail utterly, and so long as a living can be made out of it these men will stick to their farms.

One brilliant spring-like day in midwinter I came upon an old man on the footpath at some distance from the nearest house, painfully walking to and fro on a clean piece of ground with the aid of two sticks. An old farmer, past work, I thought. His appearance greatly attracted me, for though his bent shrunken legs could hardly support him, he had a fine head and a broad, deep, powerful-looking chest. His face was of that intensely Irish type so common in West Cornwall, but more shapely, more noble, with a look of strength and resolution not at all common,

Seeing that he was old I supposed he was deaf, and shouted my "Good day," and the remark that it was a very fine day. But there was no need to shout, his senses were very good. "Good day to you," he returned, his stone-grey stern eyes fixed on my face. "Yes, it is a fine day indeed—very, very fine. And no frost, no cold at all, and the winter going on, going on. We are getting on very well indeed." And to this subject he kept in spite of my attempts to lead the talk to something else. The lovely weather, the extraordinary mildness of the season, the comfort of a winter with no frost or cold at all—to that he would come back. And at length, when I said good-bye and left him, the last words I heard him say were, "Yes, the winter is going—very freely, very freely." For he was old—his age was eighty-seven; he had come to that time of life when the weather becomes strangely important to a man, when winter is a season of apprehension; when he remembers that the days of our age are three-score years and ten, and though men be so strong that they come to four-score years, yet is their strength then but labour and sorrow, so soon passeth it away. I was told that he had farmed the land where I found him taking his constitutional since he was a young man; that some months ago, on account of his infirmities, he had handed the farm over to one of his sons, and that he was still able to help a little in the work. His arms were strong still, and once up on the seat he could drive a cart or trap or reaping machine as well as anyone.

He was but one of several grey old men I met with on the farms, and it seemed to me that they were something like their neighbour the badger, that they are as tenacious of their dreary-looking little homesteads and stony fields as that tough beast is of his earth among the rocks.

OLD CORNISH HEDGES

EVERYONE in England knows what a hedge is—a row of thorn or other hardy bushes originally planted to protect a field, which, when old and unkept, has the appearance and character of a brake or thicket. It consequently comes as a surprise when we first visit the remote and most un-English county of Cornwall to discover that a hedge there may mean something quite different. It puzzled me to read in a book on Cornwall that in some exceedingly rough places near the coast one found it easier to make one's way over the ground by climbing on to a hedge and walking along its top. The oldest, toughest, closest and most evenly-cut hedge one knows would hardly afford a safe footing for a man; and as to attempting to get upon or walk on a big unkept hedge, such as are common in the south and west counties on this side the of Tamar, the very thought of it is painful. In imagination one sees, and seeing feels, oneself stuck fast in a big bramble bush. In Cornwall I discovered that a stone wall was called a hedge—the sort of wall which in Scotland I had been taught to call a dyke. I did not like it so well as the English hedge, that wild disordered tangle of all the most beautiful plants in these islands—black and white thorn; privet with its small grape-like clusters; yew and holly and ivy with late, honeyed blossoms for bees and wasps and hornets; and briar and sweet-briar, bramble and bryony; also poisonous black bryony and traveller's-joy, a green and silver tapestry; and wayfaring tree, spindlewood and cornel, with scarlet, purple and orange-coloured berries; dark deadly-nightshade, pushing its slender stems up through the interlaced branches—all massed together for common protection like a packed herd of wild swine on their defence in some savage solitude, displaying bristling backs and bared gnashing tushes to a hostile world.

They are—these wildings of the hedge—the counterparts in the vegetable world of the creatures called "vermin" in the animal kingdom.

In the recesses of their thorny intertwining boughs, and deep down among their tough ancient roots, the vermin, the banned ones, have their home and refuge—the quaint hedgehog and minute long-nosed shrew; black and white magpie and chacking, tail shaking butcher-bird; adder and snake and slow worm; blood-sucking stoat and weasel with flat heads and serpentine bodies, and their small quarry, rats and voles and pretty sharp-nosed wood-mice with leaf-like ear, and winter-sleeping dormice.

It was fortunate that in the long ago, when our progenitors began to take plots of ground for cultivation and pasture, they found out this cheap ready way of marking their boundaries and safeguarding their cattle and corn. We may say they planted better than they knew: they planted once, and many and many a hedge—unnumbered miles and leagues of hedges—that are now great belts of thicket, were first planted by man in the remote past. Nature took over the thin row of thorn seedlings and made it what it is, not only the useful thing it was intended for—a natural barbed-wire entanglement—but a thing of beauty and a joy for ever.

In West Cornwall, where I first came to know the native hedge, they cannot have these belts of thicket, rich in a varied plant and animal life. It is a country of moors and rugged stony hills where nothing flourishes but heath and furze and bracken. The farming folk have succeeded in long time in creating small arable and grass fields in the midst of this desolation, but they cannot grow trees on account of the violent winds charged with salt moisture that blow incessantly from the Atlantic. If the farmer plants a few trees so that he may one day eat an apple of his own growing and sit in the shade, he must build a wall eight or ten feet high to protect them from the salt blast, and he may then die of old age before the apple is ripe or the shade created. Nor can he grow a hedge: the furze, it is true, abounds everywhere, but it is a most intractable plant that will go (or grow) its own wild way, and no man has yet subdued it to his will and made it serve as a hedge. Yet even in this wind-vexed land a few self-planted trees may be seen.

You find them in the strip of farm country between the hills and sea, in hollows and under high banks, or where a mass of rock affords them shelter; and they are mostly hawthorns and blackthorns with a few hardy bush-like trees of other kinds. They are like the trees and bushes on the most exposed coasts in Yorkshire and in other places, growing all one way, lying close to and sometimes actually on the ground, stretching out their branches and every twig towards the inland country. The sight of these wind-tormented, one-sided trees fascinates me and I stay long to look at them.

A bristled tree
With branches cedared by the salten gale,
Stretched back, as if with wings that cannot flee,

is how Gordon Hake describes the appearance, seeing, as I do, the desire
and struggle to escape—to fly from that pitiless persecution. But the
"wings" I do not see: in summer the foliage is to my sight but a ragged
mantle; in winter the human expression is strongest and most pathetic.
Held by the feet, in the grip of earth, the beaten bush strains to get
away; it suggests the figure of a person crawling, or trying to crawl, the
knee-like joints on the ground, the body-like trunk thrown forward, the
long bare branches and terminal twigs, like the brown, thin naked arms
and claw-like opened fingers of a starving scourged slave in the tropics,
extended imploringly towards the land.

This being the nature of the country, the farmer can but hedge his land
and fields with stone: he is in a measure compelled to do so, since the earth
is full of it and the land strewn with boulders; to make a field he must
remove it and bestow it somewhere. Now after centuries of this process
of removing and piling up stones, the farm land has become covered
over with a network of these enduring hedges, or fences, intersecting
each other at all angles; and viewed from a hill-top the country has the
appearance of a patched quilt made of pieces of all sizes and every possible
shape, and of all shades of green from darkest gorse to the delicate and
vivid greens of the young winter grass.

That half-reclaimed district, especially the strip of coast from St. Ives
Bay to Cape Cornwall, was a good winter hunting-ground, and I spent
many weeks in ranging about the fields and waste or incult places among
them. Here you can wander at will, without fear of hurting the farmer's
feelings, as in Devonshire, by walking on his land. The cultivation is
little, the fields being mostly grass: the small farm house is out of sight
somewhere behind the stone hedges; it is rare to meet with a human
being, and the few cows or calves you occasionally come across follow
you about as if only too pleased to have a visitor. Climbing over the next
hedge into the next field you find nobody there but a pig who stares at
you, then welcomes you with a good-humoured grunt; or an old solitary
plough-horse; or no semi-human domestic creature at all, only a crowd
of busy starlings; or starlings mixed with daws, fieldfares, missel-thrushes
and a few wagtails; or a couple of magpies, or a small flock of wintering
curlews to be found day after day on the same spot. After crossing two
or three such fields you come upon an unreclaimed patch, or belt, where

grey-lichened rocks are mixed with masses of old furze bushes, and heath and tussocks of pale brome-grass. A lonely, silent, peaceful place, where, albeit a habitation of man for untold centuries, it is wild Nature still.

Here, with eyes and mind occupied with the birds, I did not at first pay much attention to the hedges: I simply got over them, or, in thorny and boggy places, walked on them, but eventually they began to exercise an attraction, and I began to recognise that these, too, like the planted hedges of other districts were man's creation but in part, since Nature had added much to make them what they are. Human hands first raised them: the process is going on all the time; the labourer, the cow-boy, the farmer himself, when there is nothing else to do, goes out and piles up stones to stop a gap the cattle have made, to add to the height or length of an old hedge, and so on, but the wall once made, is taken over by Nature as in the case of the planted hedge. She softens and darkens the crude harsh surface, clothes it in grey and yellow lichens and cushioned green moss, and decorates it with everything that will grow on it, before the time comes for her to ruin and finally to obliterate. But what time is needed here for demolition with such a material as granite to work on, where there are no trees to insinuate their roots into the crevices, slowly to expand the pliant fibres into huge woody wedges to thrust the loose stones apart and finally to pull them down! We can imagine how slow the destructive processes are when we look at innumerable Cornish crosses scattered over the county, showing clearly the lines cut on them in the early days of Christianity in this district. Still more do we see it in the ancient sacred stones—the cromlechs, coits, hurlers and holed stones, moor-stones or "merry maidens," and many others—which have stood and resisted the disintegrating effect of the weather since prehistoric times. The wall built is practically everlasting, but Nature works slowly on it, and the hedges I had about me differed greatly on this account, from the rude walls raised but yesterday or a dozen or twenty years ago to those which must have stood for centuries or for a thousand years or longer. Indeed, it was the appearance of extreme antiquity in one of these hedges, which I often crossed and sometimes walked on, which first excited my interest in the subject. It looked, and probably is, older than the walls of Silchester, which date back 1700 or 1800 years, and are now being gradually pulled down by the trees that have grown upon them. It was the longest of the old hedges I found, beginning among the masses of granite on the edge of the cliff, and winding away inland to lose itself eventually among the rocks and gullies and furze thickets at the foot of a great boulder-strewn hill. Its sinuosity struck me as a mark of extreme age, as in this it resembled the huge prehistoric walls or earthworks made of chalk on the downs in Southern England, which meander in an extraordinary way. It was also larger than the other hedges, which crossed its winding course at all angles, being in most parts six to seven feet high, and exceedingly broad; moreover, where the stones could be seen they appeared to be more closely fitted together than in other hedges. Most of the stonework was, however, pretty well covered over, in some places with a very thick turf, in others by furze and bracken, rooted in the crevices and in places hiding the wall in a dense thicket.

But of all the plants growing on it the ivy was most remarkable. It is not a plant that flourishes in this district, where it has as hard a struggle as any tree to maintain its existence. It is found only in sheltered situations on this coast, in the villages, and on the landward side of steep banks and large masses of rock. On this old wall there was really no shelter, since the furious blasts from the sea swept both sides of it with the same violence. Yet in places the ivy had got possession of it, but it was an ivy very much altered in character by the unfavourable conditions from that greenest luxuriant plant we know so well. In place of the dark mass of foliage, the leaves were few and small and far apart, so that viewing the wall from a little distance away you would not notice that it had any ivy growing on it, but would see that the more naked portions were covered with a growth of rope-like stems. The wonder is that with so few leaves it can grow so much wood! The stems, which are not thick, are smooth and of a pale grey colour and grow in and out of the crevices, and cross and re-cross one another, fitting into all the inequalities of the stony surface and in places where they cover the wall looking like a numerous brood or tangle of grey serpents.

This snaky appearance of the almost leafless old wall-ivy fascinated me, and I went often to look at it on the same spot and was never tired of the sight. It struck me as curious that the woody ivy should have this aspect, since the wall itself in some parts distinctly suggested the serpentine form and appearance. Here again I was reminded of some of the long earthworks or walls on the Wiltshire and Dorsetshire downs— the rounded, thickly turfed bank which winds serpent-like over the hills and across the valleys, and which often has a green colour differing slightly from that of the earth it lies across.

The old Cornish hedge had this aspect in places where it was clothed with turf, and, viewed from a distance and seen winding about in great curves across the rough brown heath and furze-grown earth, the serpentine appearance was very marked.

Whether or not the Cornish antiquaries have paid any attention to these ancient hedges I do not know. The only native I came across who had anything to say about them was a peasant farmer whose acquaintance I made at his cottage-like farm, a few miles from the hedge I have described. He was a man of seventy-nine, but vigorous still and of a lively mind.

When I spoke to him about the old hedge and its ancient appearance, he said he had known it all his life; that he was a native of a small hamlet close to the hedge, and at the age of seven, when he first took to birds'-nesting, he used to hunt along it on every summer day and came to know it as well as he knew the fence round his garden, and the walls of the cottage he lived in. It had not, he assured me, changed in the least during the last seventy or seventy-two years: it was to-day exactly what it was in his early boyhood, with thick turf and furze and bracken and woody ivy covering it in the same way in the same old places. This made him think it must be very, very old.

It seemed to me that his life, although a long one, was but a short period to measure by in such a case, that if he could have consulted his father and grandfather and his remoter ancestors back to the time when the last Cornish king was cast out by William the Bastard, they would all have given the same testimony and said that the hedge was very old when they knew it.

BOLERIUM: THE END OF ALL THE LAND

EVERY day, even in winter, if the weather be not too bad, but chiefly during the nine months from March to November, pilgrims come to this wind-swept, wave-beaten point to gaze and set their feet upon the little rocky promontory of the Land's End. It is less bold and impressive than many others of the hundred headlands at this western extremity of England between St. Ives and Mount's Bay. From this or that projecting point, commanding a view of the coastline for some distance, one may count a dozen or more of these headlands thrust out aslant like stupendous half-ruined buttresses supporting the granite walls of the cliff. They are of a sullen brown colour and rough harsh aspect, and in places have the appearance of being built up of huge square blocks of granite, and at other points they form stacks of columns as at the Giant's Causeway. The summits of these headlands are often high, resembling ruinous castles placed on projecting points of the cliff; they are confused masses of rocks of many shapes, piled loosely one upon the other, their exposed surfaces clothed over with long coarse grey lichen. Large gulls, daws and cormorants sit or stand here and there on the ledges and prominent points, the herring gulls clamorous at the sight of a human form; the restive daws quitting their stands to wheel about at intervals, rising and falling, soon to settle down again; the cormorants silent and motionless, standing erect with curved, snaky necks, like birds carved in ebony.

Stealing quietly among these hoary masses of rock you may see a very wild rabbit, and on a bright, still, winter day, if you are singularly fortunate, you may catch sight of a beast better worth seeing, a cliff fox, lying fast asleep or lightly dozing, stretched at full length on a ledge, looking intensely red in the sunshine, and very conspicuous against the hoary lichened rock. This is his home and castle, which he shares with the rabbits that know his ways, and the birds that are always just out of his reach. Thus do they live together in one house like one antagonistic family in a strange artificial harmony, and do not mix, but come and go and move about freely, and bask in the warm sunshine, and sit up to rub their long ears and whiskers, and spread out their wings to dry, and preen their feathers. Peace and quiet in their castle, while the great waves roll in to beat on its caverned walls beneath, making the earth tremble with their measured blows, covering the black rocks with dazzling white foam, and sending up a mist of spray to the summit.

At intervals between Bay and Bay, a distance of thirty miles, you come upon headlands of this type—Cape Cornwall, Gurnard's Head, Zennor Cliffs and others, to the north of Land's End, while just south of it you have the noblest rock scenery of this coast, including the stupendous cliffs of Tol-Pedn-Penwith and Treryn Dinas, with its famed Logan Stone. Bolerium itself, the narrow promontory of piled rocks of the Land's End and the flat bit of country adjoining it, is, sentiment apart, one of the least interesting points on the coast.

But the sentiment is a very great thing and interesting to observe. And this is easy, since the pilgrims mostly come by way of Penzance, distant about a dozen miles, travelling in batches of twenty-five or thirty or more, packed closely in some public conveyance; so that one has but to join the crowd and, sitting among them, watch their faces out of the corners of his eyes. They are a mixed company of men and women of all conditions, from all parts of the country, with some Americans and Colonials. It is indeed curious to see an identical feeling on faces so unlike, from the very young who do not try to conceal it, to the very aged and almost worn-out globe wanderers, who are now nearly at the end of their life's pilgrimage, and have seen pretty well all that was worth seeing on this wide earth except this one famous spot which by chance has been left to the last. And by-and-by, after travelling half a dozen miles, they find themselves in a land unlike any place they know; inhabited, for there are a few small sad-looking granite cottages and farms and hamlets, but of a rude and desolate aspect, and therefore in harmony with their emotions and preconceived ideas about the place. It is a treeless barren country, hill and moor, with furze and, brown heath interspersed with grey boulder stones, the whole dominated by the great desolate hill of Chapel Cam Brea. The travellers look out, straining their eyes to see the end; but before that comes the hilly country is left behind, and at the last it is flat and tame with a sad-looking granite-built village and the grey sea beyond. One has watched the bright eager look that expected so much fade out of the various faces; and by the time the pilgrims get down to scatter along the cliff or to go at once to their luncheon at the hotel it is pretty well all gone. And if you go back to Penzance to join the next lot, and then again, and every day for a week or a month, you will witness the same thing—the collection of unlike faces with the light of the same feeling in the eyes of all, increasing as they advance over that rude moorland country and fading out at the end to that blank look—"Is this the Land's End—is this all!"

What, then, did they expect? Wilkie Collins best answers that question in his pleasant book of rambles written more than half a century ago, when he says that the Land's End is to Cornwall what Jerusalem is to the Holy Land, the great and final object of a journey to the westernmost county of England, its Ultima Thule, where it ceases; a name that strikes us most in childhood when we learnt our geography; which fills the minds of imaginative people with visions of barrenness and solitude and dreams of some lonely promontory, the place where the last man in England will be found waiting for death at the end of the world.

That is indeed the secret of the visitor's expectant feeling and disappointment—the vague vision of a vastness and grandeur and desolateness almost preternatural, conceived in childhood, which all the experience of a long life of disillusionment has been powerless to eradicate from the mind, or to replace with a mental picture more in accord with the reality.

But if this disillusionment is plainly visible to an observer on the faces of many visitors, the books about Cornwall tell a different story; their writers would have us believe that the reality has surpassed their expectations, that their emotions of admiration and astonishment have been deeply moved. When I had been some time in Cornwall and it had taken hold of me, I sat myself down before a formidable array of books descriptive of the duchy, only to find that reading them was an exceedingly wearisome task. By-and-by I discovered something to entertain and keep me going; this was the grand business of describing the Land's End in a suitable manner, but more or less rhetorically and charged with exalted feeling, which was undertaken in turn by every visitor. This made many a dull book amusing. I experienced a kind of sporting interest in the literary traveller's progress through the county, and looked eagerly forward to his arrival at the famous spot where he would have to pull himself together and launch himself bird-like from the cliffs, as it were, on the void sublime. There was great variety in these utterances, but I think the one that diverted me most was in a book entitled *A Trip to the Far West,* published in 1840, as the author, one Baker Peter Smith, was evidently an experimenter in words, some of his own making; or we might call him an Early Victorian young man in search of a style.

"I reached the Land's End," he wrote, "and sat down on a protuberant block of granite, close to the precipice, overhanging the multitangular rocks which form an impenetrable barrier against the raging tides of the mighty waters." After lamenting that he had so little time in which to survey the "multicapsular curiosities of the region," he proceeds: "The local sublimity of the Land's End affords a commanding view of scenick expanse; and the colossal columns of rock give an awful effect to the stupendous vision; whilst, added to these grave and elevating sentiments, consequent on so grand a sight, the sense of hearing also acts upon the mind: by the distant roar of the angry sea, ascending from the caverns below, and the screaming of the Cornish chough assailing you from above and every side," and so on. He concludes: "The entranced spectator has no election, but is engrossed with admiration of that Great Power by the fiat of whose mere volition nature's chaos was thus harmonised and stamped with the glorifying impress of multiplicious beauty."

One is glad that cormorant, book-devouring Time has spared us Baker Peter Smith. But there are a few noble passages to be found as well, and I think this one of Humphry Davy, written in youth before the flower of poesy withered in him, pleases me the best:

On the sea
The sunbeams tremble and the purple light
Illumes the dark Bolerium, seat of storms!
Dear are his granite wilds, his schistine rocks
Encircled by the waves, where to the gale
The haggard cormorant shrieks, and, far beyond
Where the great ocean mingles with the sky,
Behold the cloud-like islands, grey in mist.

Another notable utterance was that of John Wesley, when on a Sunday in September, 1743, after preaching to the people at Sennen, he went down to look at the Land's End. "It was an awful sight," he wrote. "But how will this melt away when God ariseth in judgment! The sea beneath doth indeed boil like a pot. One would think the deep to be hoary. But though they swell yet can they not prevail. He shall set their bounds which they cannot pass."

There spoke the founder of Methodism, saturated in biblical phraseology until it gushed spontaneously from him even as its song or cry from a bird. He had forgotten his own language, as it were, and even in an exalted moment in this grey north land could only express himself in these old Asiatic figures of speech.

To return from this digression. Although the vague image of an imagined Land's End fades from the mind and is perhaps lost when the reality is known, the ancient associations of the place remain, and, if a visit be rightly timed, they may invest it with a sublimity and fascination not its own. I loitered many days near that spot in mid winter, in the worst possible weather, but even when pining for a change to blue skies and genial sunshine I blessed the daily furious winds which served to keep the pilgrims away, and to half blot out the vulgar modern buildings with rain and mist from the Atlantic. At dark I would fight my way against the wind to the cliff, and down by the sloping narrow neck of land to the masses of loosely piled rocks at its extra. It was a very solitary place at that hour, where one feared not to be intruded on by any other night-wanderer in human shape. The raving of the wind among the rocks; the dark ocean—exceedingly dark except when the flying clouds were broken and the stars shining in the clear spaces touched the big black incoming waves with a steely-grey light; the jagged isolated rocks, on which so many ships have been shattered, rising in awful blackness from the spectral foam that appeared and vanished and appeared again; the multitudinous hoarse sounds of the sea, with throbbing and hollow booming noises in the caverns beneath—all together served to bring back some thing of the old vanished picture or vision of Bolerium as we first imagine it. The glare from the various lighthouses visible at this point only served to heighten the inexpressibly sombre effect, since shining from a distance they made the gloomy world appear vaster. Down in the south, twenty-five miles away, the low clouds were lit up at short intervals by wide white flashes as of sheet lightning from the Lizard lights, the most powerful of all lights, the reflection of which may be seen at a distance of sixty or seventy miles at sea. In front of the Land's End promontory, within five miles of it, was the angry red glare from the Longships tower, and further away to the left the white revolving light of the Wolf lighthouse.

It was perhaps on some tempestuous winter night at the Land's End that the fancy, told as a legend or superstitious belief in J. H. Pearce's *Cornish Drolls*, occurred to him or to someone, that the Wolf Rock was the habitation of a great black dog, a terrible supernatural beast that preys on the souls of the dead. For the rock lies directly in the route of those who die on the mainland and journey over the sea to their ultimate abode, the Scilly Isles: and when the wind blows hard against them and

they are beaten down like migrating birds and fly close to the surface, he
is able as they come over the rock to capture and devour them.

During these vigils, when I was in a sense the "last man" in that most
solitary place, its associations, historical and mythical, exercised a strange
power over me. Here, because of its isolation, or remoteness, from Saxon
England, because it is the very end of the land, "the westeste point of the
land of Cornewalle," the ancient wild spirit of the people remained longest
unchanged, and retained much of its distinctive character down to within
recent times. It was a Celtic people with an Iberian strain, even as in Wales
and Ireland and Scotland. Now, either because of a different proportion
of the dark aboriginal blood, or of the infusion of Scandinavian and other
racial elements, or some other cause, these four Celtic families differ very
widely, as we know; but we think, or at all events are accustomed to say,
that they are an imaginative, a poetic people. Doubtless in Cornwall this
spirit was always weakest, since it never succeeded in expressing itself in
any permanent form; but albeit feeble it probably did exist, and in this
very district, this end of all the land, it must have lingered longest. If this
be so it is strange to think that it was perhaps finally extinguished by the
Wesley brothers—one with the poetry of the Hebrews ever on his lips,
the other with his own lyrical gift!

It may be said that in the middle of the eighteenth century the light
must have been so feeble that it would have soon expired of itself if
Methodism had not trampled out the last faint sparks; and it may also
be said that the Cornish people did not lose much, seeing that this root
had never flowered; that they had never sung and never said anything
worth remembering; while on the other hand their gain was a substantial
one, for though it imposed an ugly form of religion and ugly houses
of worship, it changed them (so the Methodists say) from brutality and
vice to what they are—a temperate, law-abiding people. But I shall have
something more to say on this subject in a later chapter.

Here among the rocks by night I think less of these moral changes, and
of other events within historical times, than of those which came before,
of which we have no certain knowledge. We can only assume that in the
successive invasions during the Bronze Age this was invariably the last
place conquered and last refuge of a beaten fugitive people.

I recall here a strange phenomenon in wild-bird life occasionally
witnessed in this district. Cornwall has a singularly mild and equable
climate, but great frosts do at long intervals invade it and reach to the
very extremity of the land: and when a cold wave, like that of the winter
of 1906–7, travels west, the birds flying for life before it advance along

the Cornish country until they come to a point beyond which they cannot go, for the affrighting ocean is before them and they are spent with hunger and cold. They come in a continuous stream, to congregate in tens of thousands, covering the cliffs and fields and stone hedges; and the villagers turn out with guns and nets and sticks and stones to get their fill of killing.

So in the dreadful past, whenever a wave of Celtic conquest swept west, the unhappy people were driven further and further from the Tamar along that tongue of land, their last refuge, but where there were no rivers and mountains to stay the pursuers, nor forests and marshes in which to hide, until they could go no further, for the salt sea was in front of them. They too, like the frost-afflicted birds, gathered in thousands and sat crowded in every headland and promontory and every stony hill summit, ever turning their worn dusty faces and glazed eyes to the east to watch for the coming of the foe—the strong, fiendish, broad-faced, blue eyed men with metal weapons in their hands, spear and sword and battle-axe.

These are the people I think about on dark tempestuous evenings in this solitary place; Bolerium is haunted by the vast ghostly multitude.

CASTLES BY THE SEA

IF "dark Bolerium" seemed best on tempestuous midwinter evenings because of the Spirit of the place, the sentiment, it was not so with the numerous other forelands along this rude coast. I haunted them by day, and the finer the weather the better I liked them. It is true that they too have dark associations from which one cannot wholly escape. The huge masses of rock rising high above the cliff on many of these promontories have the appearance of gigantic castles by the sea, and that they served as castles to the ancient inhabitants of the land we know, as in many instances the primitive earthworks, the trench and embankment raised to cut them off from the land, remain to this day. But the thought of the "dreadful past" is not so insistent in these castles, which were my houses by the sea, as at the Land's End promontory, and would almost vanish in the brilliant sunshine and in view of the wide expanse of ocean flecked with dazzling foam.

I could hardly imagine a higher pleasure than was mine on many a bright day in winter and spring, when I had the whole coast pretty well to myself and spent long hours in rambling from point to point and in gazing out on the sea from my seat on some rocky pile that crowned one of the bolder headlands.

I had heard a good deal about the beautiful colour of the sea in these parts, yet was often surprised at the sight of it. I had seen no such blues and greens on any other part of the British coast, and no such purples in the shallower waters within the caves and near the cliffs where the rocks beneath were over grown with seaweed. Where these great purple patches appeared on the pure brilliant green it was veritably, a "wine-purple sea," and looked as if hundreds of hogsheads of claret or Burgundy had been emptied into it.

But the sea and its colour and the joy of a vast expanse would not have drawn me so often to the castled forelands nor held me so long but for the birds that haunted them, seeing that this visible world is to me but a sad and empty place without wonderful life and the varied forms of life, which are in harmony with it, and give it a meaning, and a grace and beauty and splendour not its own. If there be no visible wild life, then I am like that wandering being or spirit in Montgomery's *Pelican Island*, who was alone on the earth before life was, and had no knowledge or intimation of any intelligence but its own; who roamed over the seas that tumbled round the globe for thousands and thousands of years, flying ever from its own loneliness and vainly seeking comfort and happiness in loving and being the companion of wind and cloud and wave, and day and night, and sun and moon and stars, and all inanimate things.

Sitting on a rock on the edge of one of these head lands I could watch those glorious fishers in the sea, the gannets, by the hour; but this bird is so great, being now the greatest left to us in Cornwall, or rather in the seas that wash its shores, and its habits so interesting, that I must by-and-by devote an entire chapter to it. Gulls and daws were the common species, always to be seen floating and wheeling about the promontory, a black and white company, with sharp yelping voices and hoarse and laughter-like cries; never wholly free from anxiety when I was by, never fully convinced of my peaceful intentions. Their habits are well known: I was not expecting any new discovery about them, it was simply the delight of seeing them which kept me to the crags. Sturge Moore says in a poem on *Wings*:

> That man who wishes not for wings,
> Must be the slave of care;
> For birds that have them move so well
> And softly through the air:
> They venture far into the sky,
> If not so far as thoughts and angels fly.
>
> Feather from under feather springs;
> All open like a fan;
> Our eyes upon their beauty dwell
> And marvel at the plan
> By which things made for use so rare
> Are powerful and delicate and fair.

In Calderon's celebrated drama, *Life's a Dream*, when Sigismund laments his miserable destiny, comparing it with that of the wild creatures which inhabited the forest where he is kept a prisoner, the contrast between his lot and theirs seems greatest when he considers the birds, perfect in form, lovely in colouring, graceful in their motions, and so wonderful in their faculty of flight; while he, a being with a higher nature, a greater, more aspiring soul, had no such liberty! We need not be so unhappy as the Polish prince to envy the birds their freedom. I watch and am never tired of watching their play. They rise and fall and circle, and swerve to this side and to that, and are like sportive flies in a room which has the wind-roughened ocean for a floor, and the granite cliffs for walls, and the vast void sky for ceiling. The air is their element: they float on it and are borne by it, abandoned to it, effortless, even as a ball of thistledown is borne; and then, merely by willing it, without any putting forth of strength; without a pulsation, to rise vertically a thousand feet, to dwell again and float upon an upper current, to survey the world from a greater altitude and rejoice in a vaster horizon. To fly like that! To do it all unconsciously, merely by bringing this or that set of ten thousand flight muscles into play, as we will to rise, to float, to fall, to go this way or that—to let the wind do it all for us, as it were, while the sight is occupied in seeing and the mind is wholly free! The balloons and other wretched machines to which men tie themselves to mount above the earth serve only to make the birds' lot more enviable. I would fly and live like them in the air, not merely for the pleasure of the aerial exercise, but also to experience in larger measure the sense of sublimity.

But this is a delusion, seeing that we possess such a sense only because we are bound to earth, because vast cliffs overhanging the sea and other altitudes are in some degree dangerous. At all events Nature says they are, and we are compelled to bow to her whether we know better or not. We cannot get over the instinct of the heavy mammalian that goes on the ground, whose inherited knowledge is that it is death or terrible injury to fall from a considerable height. Only so long as we are quite safe is this instinct a pleasurable one; but when we look over the edge of a sheer precipice, how often, in spite of reason, does the pleasure, the fearful joy, lose itself in apprehension! Could we know that it would not hurt us to drop off, purposely or by accident, that the air itself and a mysterious faculty in us would sustain us, that it would no more hurt us to be flung from the summit of a cliff than it would hurt a jackdaw, we should be as the bird is, without a sense of sublimity.

Daw and herring gull, the most abundant species, were but two of several kinds I was accustomed to see from the headlands, and some of the others were greater birds—the great black-backed gull, as big a gull as there is in the world, who had a rock to himself near the Land's End, where four or five couples could be seen congregated; and the shag, the cormorant which abounds most on this coast. They are heavy, ungainly flyers, and have an ugly reptilian look when fishing in the sea, but seen standing erect and motionless, airing their spread wings, they have a noble decorative appearance, like carved bird-figures on the wet black jagged rocks amid the green and white tumultuous sea. There, too, was the ancient raven, and he was the most irreconcilable of all. At one spot on the cliff close to where I was staying a solitary raven invariably turned up to shadow me. He would fly up and down, then alight on a rock a hundred yards away or more and watch me, occasionally emitting his deep hoarse human-like croak; but it failed to frighten me away or put me in a passion, as I was not a native. The Cornishman of the coast, when he hears that ominous sound, mocks the bird: "Corpse! corpse! you devil! If I had a gun I'd give you corpse!" It is not strange the raven views the human form divine with suspicion in these parts: he is much persecuted by the religious people hereabouts, and when they cannot climb up or down to his nest on a ledge of the cliff, they are sometimes able to destroy it by setting fire to a furze bush and dropping it upon the nest from above.

The rocky forelands I haunted were many, but the favourite one was Gurnard's Head, situated about midway between St. Ives and Land's End. It is the grandest and one of the most marked features of that bold coast. Seen from a distance, from one point of view, the promontory suggests the figure of a Sphinx, the entire body lying out from the cliff, the waves washing over its huge black outstretched paws and beating on its breast, its stupendous deformed face composed of piled masses of granite looking out on the Atlantic. I was often there afterwards, spending long hours sitting on the rocks of the great head and shoulders, watching the sea and the birds that live in it; and later, when April set the tiny bell of the rock pipit tinkling, and the wheatear, hovering over the crags, dropped his brief delicious warble, and when the early delicate flowers touched the rocks and turf with tender, brilliant colour, I was more enamoured than ever of my lonely castle by the sea. Forced to leave it I could but chew samphire and fill my pockets with its clustered green finger-like leaves, so as to have the wild flavour of that enchanting place as long as possible in my mouth and its perfume about me.

Now I wish only to relate an adventure which befell me on that midwinter day on the occasion of my first visit, when nothing happened and I saw nothing particular except with the mind's eye, for this was an adventure of the spirit.

It was one of those perfect days when the sun shines from an unclouded sky and the wind that raves without ceasing at last falls asleep and the whole world sleeps in the warm, brilliant light, albeit with eyes wide open like a basking snake. I was abroad early, and after wandering over a good many miles of moor and climbing several hills I arrived at my destination, tired and very hungry, and the first thing I did was to lunch heartily on bread and cheese and beer at the inn which you find at a short distance from the promontory. Naturally after my meal and an hour's scramble over the rough rocks of the headland I felt disposed to take a good rest before setting out on my return, and I soon found a suitable spot—a slab of stone lying with a slope to the sea on the edge of the crag. It was like a table-top with a rich cloth of grey and orange-coloured lichen covering it, and was very warm in the sun, and to make it more comfortable I rolled up my waterproof and put it under my head, so that lying there at full length I could still look at the sea and the gulls and gannets passing and repassing before me.

In a very few minutes I began to grow drowsy. So much the better, I thought; for never is sleep more sweet and refreshing to a tired man than when it comes to him under the wide sky on a warm day. The sensation of being overcome is itself very delightful, so I did not resist but welcomed it, albeit quite conscious that it was there in me and would soon have me in its power. In a vague way I even felt interested and amused at the process: I could imagine that the spirit of sleep was there in person, kneeling on the rock behind my head and making her passes, until the wide sea and wide sky began to seem all of one colour and the figures of the gulls and gannets to grow vaguer as they passed before me. Presently I was in that state when the mind ceases to think, when the place of thought is taken by pictures from memory, which come, as it were, floating before us to pass away, and be succeeded by others and still others without any connection. They are not "suggestions of contiguity" nor even of "analogy": they are not suggestions at all, and come we know not how or why.

Now among these visions or pictures of things seen or heard or read of there was one described in a poem called *The Hunter's Vision*, which had been lying for years unknown or forgotten in some dusty lumber-room of the brain. I read it first in my early years, and though it was poor poetry it powerfully affected me, partly because I was a hunter myself in those days, although only a boy hunter, and often wandered far into lonely places, and sometimes when faint with heat and fatigue I rested and even fell asleep in the shadow of a bush or of my own horse. The poem relates how the tired hunter at noon sat down to rest on a jutting crag on the steep mountain side where he had been climbing, and how when gazing before him the burning heavens and vast plains of earth, scorched brown by the summer sun, grew misty and dim to his sight, then gradually changed to a vision of his early home. He knew it well—the old familiar scene—and those who were assembled there to welcome him; how could he but know them—his long dead and long lost; they were there gazing at him, and some were coming with outstretched arms towards him, their faces shining with joy. The very words of the poem came back to me with the picture:

> Forward with fixed and eager eyes
> The hunter leaned in act to rise.

But he leaned too far in his eagerness and slipped from the crag and woke, if he ever woke at all, to know for one brief, bitter moment that he was lost for ever.

It is a story to be told, whether in verse or prose, in the simplest, directest manner; for is there a more poignant grief than that of the lonely, weary man, especially in some solitary place, who remembers his loneliness, that he is divided by death and change and absence from his own kin who were dearer than all the world to him? And just as his thought is the saddest, so the dream of a return to and reunion with the lost ones is assuredly the most blissful he can know.

Now, on the verge of sleep, seeing that picture pass before me—the ineffable sadness of the lonely hunter in the wilderness, the vision, the unutterable joy, and the fearful end—I thought (for thought now came to me) of my own case—my loneliness, for I, too, was lonely, not because I was there by myself on that promontory, but because a whole ocean and the impassable ocean of death separated me from my own people. Then it came into my mind that I, too, fast falling into oblivion, would experience that blissful vision; that the hoarse sound of the sea far below on the rocks would sink and change to the sound of the summer wind in the old poplars, that I would see the old roof and all those I first knew and loved on the earth—see them as in the old days "returned in beauty from the dust," and seeing them should start forward "in act to rise," and so end my wanderings by falling from that sloping, perilous rock!

In a moment I became wide awake, for I did not wish to perish by accident just yet, and, jumping up, I stretched out my arms, stamped with my feet, and rubbed my eyes vigorously to get rid of my drowsiness; then sat down quietly and resumed my watch of gulls and gannets.

THE BRITISH PELICAN

"BRITISH pelican" may seem almost too grand a name for a bird the size of our gannet, or Solan goose; but he is of that family, and was once, in the Linn classification, of the very genus—a *Pelicanus*. Moreover, in this land of small birds—thanks to the barbarians who have extirpated the big ones—the *Sula bassana* is very large, being little inferior to the goose, though he is certainly small compared with his magnificent rose-coloured relation, the greatest of the true pelicans.

Until I came to Cornwall I never had a proper opportunity of observing this noble fowl and his fishing methods; here he is common all round the coast, especially in the winter months, and when, as frequently happens, he fishes close to the land, he may be watched very comfortably by the hour from a seat on some high foreland. A rock two or three hundred feet above the sea is the very best position for the spectator; the birds float to and fro almost on a level with his eyes, and their beautiful motions can be better seen than from a boat or ship.

Standing on the yellow sands in the little cove behind St. Ives I watched the tide coming in one rough cloudy evening, the sea as it advanced rising into big glassy billows of a clear glaucous green colour before bursting in foam and spray running far and wide over the pale smooth sandy floor. Close behind the advancing waves a number of birds were flying to and fro, mostly herring gulls, but there were also a good many gannets. These moved up and down in a series of wide curves at a rate of speed which never varied, with two or three or four beats of the powerful, pointed, black-tipped white wings, followed by a long interval of gliding; the bird always keeping at a height of about twenty-five feet above the surface, and, without an instant's pause or hesitation, dashing obliquely into the sea after its prey.

That is how they fish sometimes, flying low and seeing the fishes a good distance ahead, and is but one of several methods. When next I was

watching them their manner was very different. The air was calm and
clear and full of bright sunlight, and I watched them from the stupendous
mass of rock forming the headland on which stands the famous Logan
Rock. The birds were in considerable numbers, sweeping round in great
curves and circles at a uniform height of about two hundred and fifty feet
from the surface. They were distributed over an immense area; ranging,
in fact, over the entire visible sea, from those that fished within a couple
of hundred yards off the rocks on which I sat, to the furthest away, which
appeared as moving white specks on the horizon. When fishing from that
height the gannet drops straight down on its prey, striking the sea with
such force as to send up a column of water eight or ten feet high, the bird
disappearing from sight for a space of five or six seconds, or longer, then
rising and after floating a few moments on the surface rising laboriously
to resume its flight as before. The fall of the big white bird from such
a height is a magnificent spectacle, and causes the spectator to hold his
breath as he watches it with closed wings hurl itself down as if to certain
perdition. The tremendous shock of the blow on the sea would certainly
kill the bird but for the wad of dense elastic plumage which covers and
protects it. For it hits itself as hard as it hits the sea, and how hard that is
we may know when we watch the gannet drop perpendicularly like a big
white stone, and when at a distance of a quarter of a mile we can see the
column of water thrown up and distinctly hear the loud splash. Yet no
sooner has it hurled itself into the sea than it is out again as if nothing had
happened, ready for another fall and blow!

One wonders how, when the gannet is flying high, on catching sight
of a fish directly beneath him in the water, he is able instantly to check
his course, get into position and fall just at the right spot. One would
suppose that he could not do it, that the impetus of so heavy a body
moving swiftly through the air would carry him many yards beyond the
spot, and that he would have to return and search again. He does not,
in fact, bring himself to a sudden stop as the small light kestrel is able to
do, nor does he, I think, keep the fish all the time in his eye, but he is
nevertheless able to accomplish his purpose, and in this way: the instant
a fish is detected the bird shoots up a distance of a dozen to twenty
feet; thus the swift motion is not arrested, but its direction changed from
horizontal to vertical, and this is probably brought about by a lightning-
quick change in the set of the wing feathers; but it is a change which
the eye cannot detect, even with the aid of the most powerful binocular.
The upward movement is not exactly vertical; it describes a slight curve,
and, at the top, when the impetus which carried him up has spent itself,

the bird wheels round, turning half over and bringing his head down pointing to the sea. I suppose that he then quickly recovers the fish he had lost sight of for a moment, for with a pause of scarcely a second he then closes his wings and lets himself fall.

On this calm, bright day, with scores of birds in sight, I was well able to observe this beautiful aerial manoeuvre—a sort of looping the loop, and seemingly an almost impossible feat which they yet accomplish with such apparent ease.

The spectacle of many gannets fishing, all moving in a perpetual series of curves, wavering lines and half-circles, at exactly the same altitude, and all performing the same set of actions on spying a fish, produces the idea that they are automata moved by extraneous forces, and are incapable of varying their mode of action. As a fact, they vary it constantly according to the state of the atmosphere and the sea, and probably also the depth at which the fish are swimming. But whatever the method for the day may be, one is impressed and amazed at the marvellous energy of the bird, and this strikes us most when we see gannets and gulls together.

The gull is a waiter on the tide, and on wind and rain and sunshine and any change which may bring him something to eat—a sort of feathered Mr. Micawber among sea-birds. His indolent happy-go-lucky way of making a living reminds you of his friend the fisherman who, when not fishing, can do nothing but lounge on the quay with his hands in his pockets, or stand leaning against a sunny wall revolving the quid in his mouth and making an occasional remark to the idler nearest to him. His brief and furious fits of activity are followed by long intervals of repose, when he floats at the will of wind and wave on the sea or sits dozing on a rock. He also spends a good deal of his time in a kind of loitering, probably waiting for something to turn up, when he is seen in a loose company scattered far and wide about the sea, one here, two or three a little distance off, and a few more a hundred yards away; others flying about in an aimless way, dropping down at intervals as if to exchange remarks with those on the water, then wandering off again.

One day sitting on a rock at Gurnard's Head, I watched a company of forty or fifty gannets fishing in a calm sea where a great many herring and lesser black-backed gulls were scattered about idly rocking on the surface in their usual way. The gannets were sweeping round at a height of about a hundred feet, and were finding fish in plenty as their falls into the sea were pretty frequent. The gulls saw nothing, or knew that the fishes were not for them, and they were consequently not in the least excited. By-and-by I saw a gannet drop upon the sea just where two gulls were floating, sending a cloud of spray over one bird and causing both to rock and toss about like little white boats in a whirlpool. I could imagine one of those gulls gasping with astonishment and remarking to his fellow: "That was a nice thing, wasn't it! Coming down on me like that without a by-your-leave! I suppose if the fish had been swimming right under me he would have run me through with his confounded beak; and when he had shaken me off and seen me floating dead on the water, he would have said that it served me jolly well right for getting in his way! Certainly these gannets are the greatest brutes out—but what fishers!—and what splendid fellows!"

Gulls are all robbers by instinct, but have not the power and courage of the predaceous bonxie or great skua of the Shetlands, a pirate by profession who lives mainly on the labours of others. The gull must fend for himself and levy tribute when he gets the chance, when he can intimidate some other bird or snatch a morsel from his beak. From the gannet he gets nothing; it would be dangerous for him to come in that bird's way, and no sooner is the fish caught than it is swallowed. The gannet takes no more notice of the gull than of a bubble floating on the surface, and probably does not even know that the negligible bird regards his fishing operations with a good deal of interest and hungrily wishes he could have a share in the spoil. But how far gulls will go in their desire to get something for nothing may be seen in the following incident which was witnessed by some fishermen at Sennen Cove, close to the Land's End. A great northern diver made its appearance at the cove and spent a part of the winter there, and as he was not disturbed and grew accustomed to the sight of human beings he lost all shyness and often fished close to the rocks where the men stood watching him. One day they saw him with a small flat-fish which he could not swallow; it was top broad to go down his gullet, but he would not let it escape and continued to toss it up and catch it again, as if determined to get it down somehow. Or it may have been that he was only playing with it just as a cat when not hungry plays with a mouse. By and by a black-backed gull swam to him and began following him and making snatches at the flounder each time the diver tossed it up. But the diver would not let him have the fish, he simply turned round to get away from the teasing gull, and the quiet way in which he took it only emboldened the other until he became quite excited and was almost violent in his efforts to get the fish. Then suddenly the diver, dropping the fish, turned on him and struck him like lightning, driving his sharp powerful beak into his neck or the base of the skull. The gull flapped his wings violently once or twice, then turned over and floated away, belly up, quite dead. Instantly after dealing the blow, the diver went down and quickly reappeared with the flounder, and resumed tossing and catching it again, just as if nothing had happened, while the dead gull slowly drifted further and further away.

What struck the men who witnessed the tragic incident as most remarkable was the sudden change in the temper of the diver, when he turned at last on the other, dealt him the swift killing blow, then immediately returned to his play with the fish as if the slaying of that big formidable bird had affected him no more than it would have done to shake off a drop of water. My thought on hearing about it was that the act of the diver was wonderfully like that of many a human being to whom killing is no murder, who kills in a casual way because of some religious or ethical or political idea, or merely because he has been annoyed or stung into a fit of anger, and who, the killing done, recovers his normal placid temper and thinks no more about it.

An exceedingly painful incident of this kind is related by Darwin in describing the natives of Tierra del Fuego in his *Voyage of a Naturalist*. Another very pathetic case is related by Browning, in the *Dramatic Idylls*, in which the woodcutter in a Russian village who is able to handle his axe so deftly strikes off the head of a young woman who has just escaped from the wolves that pursued her in the forest. They sprang upon her in her sleigh and dragged her child from her arms; the pious woodcutter thought she should have allowed herself to be torn to pieces before releasing the child. Then, after striking her head off he goes to his cottage, puts down the axe, and plays with his children on the floor, and is greatly surprised that any fuss should be made by his fellow-villagers at what he had done.

The gulls have a particularly uncomfortable time when, as occasionally happens during the pilchard fishing, a number of gannets appear to claim their share in the spoil. No sooner has the circle of the seine been completed, forming a pool teeming with fish in the sea as it were, than the gulls are there in a dense crowd. Then if the gannets appear hovering over them and hurling themselves down like rocks into the seine, the gulls scatter in consternation and have to wait their turn. The wonder is that the gannets, diving with such violence, bird following bird so closely, all in so small an area, do not collide and kill each other. Somehow as by a miracle they escape accidents, and when they have gorged until they can gorge no more they retire to digest their meal at sea, and immediately the gulls return to feast with a tremendous noise and much squabbling, each bird fighting to deprive his neighbour of the fish he picks up. This lasts until the gannets, having quickly digested their first meal or got rid of it by drinking sea-water, return with a fresh appetite for a second one, and the poor gulls are once more compelled to leave that delectable spot, teeming and glittering with myriads of rushing, leaping, terrified pilchards.

At other times, when fishing-birds are attracted to one spot by shoals of mackerel, herring, sprats or pilchards, gulls and gannets feast together very comfortably, and as the gulls take good care not to get in the way of their too energetic neighbours, there are probably no accidents. Occasionally at such times they have an opportunity of feeding on the launce or sand-eel, a favourite food of all the rapacious creatures, fish and fowl, that get their living in the sea. The launce is a long slender eel-like silvery fish that has the curious habit of burying itself in the sand, and it is said that when out feeding if pursued it instinctively darts down to the bottom of the sea to escape by burying itself in the sand. Bass and pollack are the greatest persecutors of the launce, and when a number of these greedy fishes come upon a shoal of sand-eels in deep water they get beneath them to hold them up, and surround them as well to prevent their escape. Day, in his *British Fishes*, states that pollack have been observed acting in this way on the coast of Norway; but many Cornish fishermen have witnessed it too, though it has not been described by Jonathan Couch and other writers on the habits of the native fishes as occurring in our waters. A native of Hayle, a boatman and a keen observer of bird and fish life, gave me the following account of a scene he witnessed in St. Ives Bay, not far from the Godrevy Lighthouse. His attention was attracted by a great concourse of gulls and gannets, and rowing to the spot he found the surface of the sea boiling with an immense shoal of sand-eels rushing about on the surface and clean out of the water in their efforts to escape from their pursuers. It was a very unusual sight, as the shoals of sand-eels are usually small, but here they swarmed at the surface over a very large area—probably six or seven acres. It was a fine, bright day and the water being marvellously clear he could see the pollack ranging swiftly about at a considerable depth and rising at intervals to the surface to capture their prey. Meanwhile the birds in hundreds were hovering overhead, the gannets coming down in their usual way like huge stones hurled into the sea, the gulls swooping lightly and snatching their prey and rising with the long silvery wriggling fishes in their beaks.

Every gull thus rising with a launce in its beak was of course instantly pursued and set upon by all the others flying near, and had to fight furiously to retain his capture.

That is invariably the gull's way: even when fish are swarming on the surface and easily taken they must give vent to their predatory instincts and waste time and energy in robbing one another and in squabbling and screaming, instead of every bird trying to catch as many as he can for himself. It is very different with the gannet; he never in all his life—and it may be a life of a century or longer for all we know to the contrary—wastes as much energy as would be the equivalent of a single feather's weight in trying to take a morsel out of the beak of another gannet or bird of any kind. One might say that his faculties are so perfect, his power so great, that he has no need to descend to such courses. Indeed, so admirably is he fitted for his sea life, that when we view him in very bad weather, when he is travelling, following the coastline, in an everlasting succession of beautiful curves and wave-like risings and failings; and when he is fishing, even when the sky is black with tempests and the tumbling ocean is all grey and white with whirling spindrift; when the furious wind has blown the whole tribe of gulls inland many a league, he appears to us as a part of it all—of wave and spray and wind and cloud—a fragment, one of a million, torn away by the blast, into which a guiding spirit or intelligent principle or particle has been blown to make it cohere and give it form and weight and indestructibility.

I can but express it in my blundering fashion, but the thought has been in my mind when, sitting on a rock on some high foreland, I have watched the gannets passing by the hour, travelling to some distant feeding area. or to their breeding haunts in the far north; a procession many a league long, but a very thin procession of twos and twos, every bird with his mate, following the trend of the coast, each bird in turn now above the sea, now down in the shelter of a big incoming wave, and every curve and every rise and fall of one so exactly repeated by the other as to give the idea of a bird and its shadow or reflection, with bird and reflection continually changing places.

After seeing the gannet every day for months one would be apt to think that this species is incapable of making a mistake and is beyond reach of accidents, but that cannot be supposed of any living creature, however perfect the correspondence may appear between it and the environment. At Sennen I heard of an extraordinary mishap which befell and caused the destruction of a large number of gannets. It was told to me by several of the fishermen who witnessed it at Sennen Cove, at the Land's End, and by a gentleman of the place, who is a keen ornithologist and was present at the time. A strong wind was blowing straight into the bay, and there was a very big sea on. The sea, they told me, presented a singular appearance on account of the enormous waves rolling in; the village people, in fact, were all out watching it. A large number of gannets were busy fishing and were coming further and further in, following the shoal. Then a wonderful thing happened on this day of wonders; the wind which had been blowing a gale fell quite suddenly and was succeeded in a very few minutes by a perfect calm. Some of the men assured me they had never known such a thing happen before. I have known it once, and that was in South America, when a violent south-west wind which had been blowing for many hours dropped suddenly, and the air was a dead calm before the loud noise of the gale in the trees was out of my ears. The change was disastrous to the gannets; in that windless atmosphere in the sheltered bay and with the sea in that state they could not rise. They were seen struggling on the water and carried shorewards by the huge incoming waves; but their fellows flying to and fro above them, intent on their prey, did not see or heed their distress; they continued dashing down into the sea, bird after bird, and every one that hurled itself down remained down, until they were all in the sea, all vainly flapping and struggling to keep out and still being carried nearer and nearer to the shore. Then the waves began to fling them out on the flat sandy beach, and as wave followed wave, bringing more and more of the birds, the men and boys who were watching went mad with excitement and set off at a run, every one as he went snatching up a stick or an iron bar or whatever would serve as a weapon. There was no escape for the birds, for their wings could not lift them, and they were slaughtered without mercy, even as shipwrecked men on this dreadful coast in the ancient days had been slaughtered, and the sands were covered with their carcasses. The ancient wreckers got something from the unhappy wretches they slew, but these people got nothing from the gannets. I asked them why they slew the birds, and they could only shrug their shoulders or answer that they had the birds cast out by the sea at their mercy—what was there to do but to kill them? And it was added that after all, being dead, they did serve some good purpose, for by-and-by a farmer came and carried them away by cartloads to manure his land.

BIRD LIFE IN WINTER

A GOOD deal of space has already been given to the sea-birds of this coast, but the landbirds deserve a chapter too. I do not wish, however, to give an account or a list of all of them, but would rather follow Carew's example, and note only "such as minister some particular cause of remembrance." The reader who would have more than this must seek for it in one of those "hasty schedules or inventories of God's property made by some clerk"—the local ornithologies and lists of species in the Victorian and other histories and various other works. On this exposed, wind-beaten, treeless coast country one does not expect to find an abundant or varied bird life; nevertheless in this unpromising place and in winter I had altogether a very pleasant time with the feathered people.

When the weather was too bad for the cliffs the gulls were driven inland. Gannets and cormorants could endure it; the sea was their true home and abiding-place and they were not to be torn from it; but the vagrant, unsettled and somewhat unballasted gulls would not or could not stay, and were like froth of the breakers which is caught up and whirled inland by the blast. On such days (and they were many) the gulls were all over the land, wandering about in their usual aimless manner, or in flocks seen resting on the grass in the shelter of a stone wall, or mixing loosely with companies of daws, rooks, pewits and other skilful worm and grub hunters, waiting idly for the chance of snatching a morsel from a neighbour's beak.

I was a little like the gulls in my habits: on fine days the cliffs and cliff castles were my favourite haunts; in very rough weather my rambles were mostly away from the sea, where I had my old companions of the sea wall, the gulls and daws, still with me. So much has already been said of this last species in former chapters that I might appear to be giving him too great prominence to bring him in again. Yet I must do so just to relate a little scene I witnessed in which this bird had a principal part, the other characters being donkeys.

The donkey is almost the only domestic creature one meets with out on the rough high moor and among the stony hills. Cows and horses are occasionally seen, but they do not strike one as native to the place as the donkey does. He is a sort of link between the homestead and the wilderness. The donkey is man's poor, patient, anciently-broken creature, but when he roams abroad in quest of that tough and juiceless fodder on the desolate heath and hillsides—a food thought good enough for the likes of him, or the likes of he, as his master would say—he fits into the scene as the cow and horse certainly do not. He is not so big, and his rough, dirty or dusty coat of dull indeterminate greys and earthy and heather-like browns makes him harmonise with his surroundings. His long-drawn reiterated droning and whistling cry strikes one, too, as a voice of the wild incult places. On this account I have a very friendly feeling for him, and was always pleased at meeting with donkeys in my solitary walks, which was often enough, as most persons keep one or more in these parts. He is a good servant, and costs nothing to keep. Frequently I turn aside to speak to them, and as a rule they turn their backs or hinder parts on me, as much as to say that they have enough of human beings in the village: here they prefer to be left alone. But when I produce an apple from my pocket they at once think better of it, and gather round me very much interested in the apple, and quite willing for the sake of the apple to let me rub their noses and pull their ears.

One day, walking softly through a thicket of very high furze bushes, I came to a small green open space in which were three donkeys, one lying stretched out full length on the bed of moss with a jackdaw sitting on his ribs busily searching for ticks or parasites of some kind and picking them from his skin. The other two donkeys were standing by, gazing at the busy bird and probably envying their comrade his good luck. My sudden appearance at a distance of two or three yards greatly alarmed them. Away flew the daw, and up jumped the recumbent donkey, and then all three stared at me, not at all pleased at the intrusion.

It seemed to me on this occasion that in the daw, the friend and helper of our poor slave the donkey, the bird that in its corvine intelligence and cunning approaches nearest to ourselves among the avians, we have yet another link uniting man to his wild fellow-creatures.

There is a good deal of rough weather but little frost in this district; behind the cliffs, sheltered by stone hedges and thickets of furze, the green field is the chief feeding-ground of the birds; there with the rooks and daws and gulls and pewits you find fieldfares—the bluebird of the natives—and missel thrushes in flock and the greybird, as the song-thrush is called, the blackbird and small troops of wintering larks. Most abundant is the starling, a winter visitor too, for he does not breed in this part of Cornwall. You will find a flock in every little field, and the sight of your head above the stone wall sends them off with a rush, emitting the low guttural alarm note which sounds like running water.

The yellowhammer is a common resident species here. We usually think him an uninteresting bird on account of his phlegmatic disposition and monotonous song, but in this district, in winter, I found him curiously attractive, and among the modestly coloured birds that were his neighbours he was certainly the most splendid. That may appear a word better suited to the golden oriole, but I am thinking of one of his aspects, as I frequently saw him, and of a miracle of the sun. Here, in winter, he congregates in small companies or flocks at the farms, and at one small farm where there was a rather better shelter than at most of the others, owing to the way the houses and outhouses and ricks were grouped together, the company of wintering yellowhammers numbered about eighty or ninety. Every evening, when there was any sun, these birds would gather on some spot—a rick or barn roof or on the dark green bushes—sheltered from the sea wind, where they could catch the last rays. Sitting motionless grouped together in such numbers they made a strangely pretty picture.

One evening, at another farm-house, I was standing out of doors talking with the farmer, when the sun came out beneath a bank of dark cloud and shone level on the slate roof of a cow-house near us. It was an old roof on which the oxidised slate had taken a soft blue-grey or dove colour—the one beautiful colour ever seen in weathered slate; and no sooner had the light fallen on it than a number of yellow-hammers flew from some other point where they had been sitting and dropped down upon this roof. They were scattered over the slates, and, sitting motionless with heads drawn in and plumage bunched out, they were like golden images of birds, as if the sun had poured a golden-coloured light into their loose feathers to make them shine.

The grey wagtail and the goldfinch, in small numbers, both beautiful birds, were wintering here, but they could not compare with those transfigured yellowhammers I had seen.

As for the vulgar sparrow, nothing—not even the miracle-working sun—could make him brilliant or beautiful to look at, and I have indeed acquired the habit of not looking and not seeing the undesired thing.

That is, in the country: in London it is different there I can be thankful for the sparrow where he does us (and the better birds) no harm and lives very comfortably on the crumbs that fall from our tables. Yet now, at one spot on this coast, I was surprised into paying particular attention to the sparrows on account of a winter custom they had acquired.

One day on very rough land, half a mile from the cliff, I came on a piece of ground of about two acres in extent surrounded by a big stone hedge, without gap or gate. It was the site of an old tin-mine abandoned fifty or sixty years ago and walled round to prevent the domestic animals from the neighbouring farms falling into the pits. It was strange that so much trouble had been taken for such an object, as in all the other disused mining pits I had come upon in the district the holes had simply been covered over with wood and big stones, or they remained open and the cattle were left to take their chance. The stone hedge was covered with a thick growth of furze, and the ground inside, protected as it was from the cattle and sheltered by the wall from the furious winds, had become a dense and in places impenetrable thicket of blackthorn, bramble, furze and ivy. So close did the blackthorn bushes grow with their upper branches tightly interwoven that it would have been possible to walk on the top of the thicket at a height of twelve or fourteen feet from the ground without the foot slipping through. There were three pits, and one, very much enlarged owing to the quantity of earth which had fallen in, was entirely occupied with a big elder bush, or tree—a curiosity in this treeless district. It was rooted in the side of the pit about fourteen feet below the surface, and its whole height was about thirty feet. Near the root the trunk divided into three great branches, or boles, and on the middle one there was an old magpie's nest on a level with my shoulders and a little beyond the reach of my hand. The birds were perhaps wise to build in such a place, since a boy could not easily rob it without danger of falling into the pit.

On going to this walled-in thicket one evening I observed a vast concourse of sparrows. They were sitting on the bushes in thousands, and more birds in small companies of a dozen or so, and in small flocks of fifty to a hundred, were continually arriving and settling down among the others to add their voices to the extraordinary hubbub they kept up. It was like a starlings' winter roosting-place, and the birds must have come from all the homesteads on either side for a good many miles. These birds, I found, roosted in the old pits, and when they had all disappeared from sight and the loud noise of chirruping had died into silence I walked up to one of the pits and stood over it. The birds took alarm and began to issue out, coming up in rushes of several hundreds at a time, rush succeeding rush at intervals of a few seconds while I stood by, but when I retired to some distance the birds would come up in a continuous stream which sometimes looked in the fading light like a column of smoke rising from the ground.

Three months later, when the sparrows were breeding and spending their nights at home, I revisited the spot, and going to the pit with the elder tree growing in it had a fresh look at the old magpie nest. And there was Mag herself, sitting on her pretty eggs under her roof of thorny sticks! After suffering my presence for about two minutes she slipped off and went away without a sound. Wishing her good luck I came away, as I did not want to make her unhappy by too long a visit.

The magpie is extremely common in these parts although there are no trees for them to breed in. You meet with him twenty times a day when out walking. He flies up a distance ahead, rising vertically, and hovers a moment to get a good look at you, then hastens away on rapidly-beating wings and slopes off into the furze bushes, displaying his open graduated tail. He haunts the homestead and is frequently to be seen associating with the poultry; there are no pheasants here and no gamekeepers to shoot him, and, as in Ireland, the people do not like to injure though they do not love him.

If you chance to hear a bird note or phrase that is new to you in this place you may be sure the magpie is its author. Like the jay he is an inventor of new sounds and has a somewhat different language for every part of the country; The loud brisk chatter, his alarm note, which resembles the tremulous bleat of a goat, is always the same; but his ordinary language, used in conversation, when he is with his mate or a small party of friends, is curiously varied and full of surprises. It was one of my amusements in genial days in winter when a confabulation was in progress to steal as near as I could and sit down among the bushes to listen.

On one such occasion, where the furze was very thick and high, I discovered that the bushes all round me teemed with minute, shadowy-looking bird-forms silently hopping and flitting about. They were golden-crested wrens wintering in this treeless place in considerable numbers. Some of the small boys I talked to in this neighbourhood knew the bird as the "Golden Christian Wrennie"—a rather pretty variant.

But the Golden Christian Wrennie is not *the* wren—not the Cornish wren; for there is a proper Cornish wren, even as there is a St. Kilda wren, and as there is a native wren, or local race of *Troglodytes parvulus*, in every county, in every village and farm-house and wood and coppice and hedge in the United Kingdom. He is a home-keeping little bird, and when you find him, summer or winter, in town or country, you know that he is a native, that his family is a very old one in that part and was probably settled there before the advent of blue-eyed man and the dawn of a Bronze Age.

He is universal, and that gives one the idea that he is very evenly distributed; but I had no sooner set foot in this "westest" part of all England than I found the wren more common than in any other part of the country known to me, and this greatly pleased me because of my love of him. Indeed, it was the prevalence of the wren which made the West Cornwall bird life seem very much to me, despite the fact that the best species have been extirpated or driven away and that no peregrine or chough or hoopoe, or other distinguished feathered stranger, can return to these shores and not be instantly massacred by the sportsmen, ornithologists and private collectors. But the common little wren is admired and respected by everyone, even by the philistines. It is not that he seeks to ingratiate himself with us like the robin; he is the very opposite of that friendly little creature, and indeed I like him as much for his independence as for his other sterling qualities. You may feed the birds every day in cold weather and have them gather in crowds to gobble up your scraps, but you will not find the wren among them. He doesn't want of your charity, and can get his own living in all seasons and in all places, rough or smooth, as you will find if you walk round the coast from St. Ives to Land's End or to Mount's Bay. Not a furze clump, nor stone hedge, nor farm building, nor old ruined tin-mine, nor rocky head land, but has its wren, and go where you will in this half-desert silent place you hear at intervals his sharp strident note; but not to welcome you. Your heavy footsteps have disturbed and brought him out of his hiding-place to look at you and vehemently express his astonishment and disapproval. And having done so he vanishes back into seclusion and dismisses the fact of your existence from his busy practical little mind. He is at home, but not to you. 'Tis the only home he knows and he likes it very well, finding his food and roosting by night and rearing his young just in that place, with fox and adder and other deadly creatures for only neighbours. Such a mite of a bird with such small round feeble wings and no more blood in him than would serve to wet a weasel's whistle! Best of all it is to see him among the rude granite rocks of a headland, living in the roar of the sea: when the wind falls or a gleam of winter sunshine visits earth you will find him at a merry game of hide-and-seek with his mate among the crags, pausing from time to time in his chase to pour out that swift piercing lyric which you will hear a thousand times and never without surprise at its power and brilliance.

In these waste stony places, where the wren is common, another small feathered creature was with me just as often—the anxious, irresolute meadow pipit, or titlark, who is the very opposite in character to the brisk, vigorous, positive little brown bird whose mind is made up and who does everything straight off. Nevertheless he gave me almost as much pleasure, only it was a somewhat different feeling—a pleasure of a pensive kind with something of mystery in it. He did not sing, even on those bright days or hours in January, which caused such silent ones as the corn bunting and pied wagtail to break out in melody. The bell-like tinkling strain he utters when soaring up and dropping to earth is for summer only: it is that faint fairy-like aerial music which you hear on wide moors and commons and lonely hillsides. In winter, he has no language but that one sharp sorrowful little call, or complaint, the most anxious sound uttered by any small bird in these islands. It is a sound that suits the place, and when the wind blows hard, bringing the noise of the waves to your ears, and the salt spray; when all the sky is one grey cloud, and sea mists sweep over the earth at intervals, blurring the outline of the hills, that thin but penetrative little sad call seems more appropriate than ever and in tune with Nature and the mind. The movements, too, of the unhappy little creature have a share in the impression he makes; he flings himself up, as it were, before your footsteps out of the brown heath, pale tall grasses and old dead bracken, and goes off as if known away by the wind, then returns to you as if blown back, and hovers and goes to this side, then to that, now close to you, a little sombre bird, and anon in appearance a mere dead leaf or feather whirled away before the blast. During the uncertain flight, and when, at intervals, he drops upon a rock close by, he continues to emit the sharp sorrowful note, and if you listen it infects your mind with its sadness and mystery. You can imagine that the wind-blown feathered mite is not what it seems, a mere pipit, but a spirit of that place in the shape and with the voice of a mournful little bird—a spirit that cannot go away nor die, nor ever forget the unhappy things it witnessed in pity and terror long ages gone when an ancient people, or a fugitive remnant, gathered at this desolate end of all the land—a tragedy so old that it was forgotten on the earth and those who had part in it turned to dust thousands of years ago.

THE PEOPLE AND THE FARMS

ONE afternoon I watched the gambols and mock fights of three ravens among the big boulder stones at a spot a little way back from the cliff, and seeing a man occupied in pulling up swedes in a field not very far off, I thought I would go and speak to him about the birds, as they haunted the spot regularly and he would perhaps be able to tell me if they ever bred in the neighbouring cliffs. I knew the man by sight, also that he was a native of the place and never in his fifty odd years had been further than about ten miles away from it. He called himself a "farmer," being the tenant of a small holding of about a dozen or fifteen acres and a small cottage which was the "farm-house." He was a curious-looking undersized man with a small narrow wizened face, small cunning restless eyes of no colour, and reddish-yellow eyebrows, perpetually moving up and down. He reminded me of an orang-utan and at the same time of a wild Irishman of a very low type.

I talked to him about the ravens, pointing to them, and he, presently recalling I dare say some exciting adventure he had met with in connection with the birds, began to tell me the strangest story I had ever listened to. It was absolutely unintelligible; the strangeness was in his manner of delivering it. He grinned and he grimaced, swinging his long thin sinewy monkey-like arms about, jerking his body, and making many odd gestures, while pouring out a torrent of gibberish, interspersed with Caffre-like clicks and other inarticulate sounds; then throwing himself back he stared up at me, wrinkling his forehead, winking and blinking, as much as to say "Now what do you think of that?"

"Yes, just so; dear me! very wonderful!" I returned; and then, after treating me to another torrent, he threw himself back on his swedes and I walked off.

I discovered that this little man, who, when excitedly talking and gesticulating, was hardly like a human being, was one of a type which

is not excessively rare on this coast. He differed from others of his kind
whom I met only in his reddish colour. The proper colour of this kind is
dark. On the St. Ives beach I one day saw another specimen. He was in
the middle of an altercation with a carter who was loading his cart with
dogfish which the fish-buyers had turned up their noses at, and so it had
to be sold for manure. He was in a state of intense excitement, dancing
about on the sands and discharging a torrent of wild gibberish at the
other. I remarked to a young Cornishman who was standing there looking
on and listening, that I could not understand a word and could hardly
believe that all the man's jabber really meant anything. "I can understand
him very well," said the young man: "he is talking *proper Cornish*."

At Sennen Cove I came upon yet another example: he too was in a
dancing rage when I first saw him, chattering, screeching and gesticulating
more like a frenzied monkey than a human being. The man he was
abusing was a big stolid fisherman, who stood with his hands in his
trouser pockets, a clay pipe in his mouth, perfectly unmoved, like a post:
it was a wonderful contrast and altogether a very strange scene.

This small, dark, peppery man, who is found throughout the country,
and whose chief characteristics appear to be intensified in West Cornwall,
is no doubt a survival or, more properly speaking, a reversion to a very
ancient type in this country. At all events, there is a vast difference
between this little blackie or brownie of Bolerium and the prevailing
type. The man of the ordinary type is medium-sized and has a broad
head, high cheek-bones, light hair, and grey-blue eyes. The "recognised
authorities" are not, I imagine, wholly to be trusted on the question of
colour: the southern half of Hampshire appears to me more of a dark
or black province than Cornwall. Probably the author of the noble
epic, *The Dawn in Britain*, was misled by the anthropologists when he
made his Cornishmen who came to the war against the Roman a dark
people:

> Who came, strange island people, to the war,
> Men bearded, bearing moon-bent shields, unlike,
> Of a dark speech, to other Britons are
> Belerians, workers in the tinny mines
> Of Penrhyn Gnawd, which Bloody Foreland named,
> Decit their king upleads them, now in arms.

At Calleva, in which the Romans were besieged by the Britons, in Book
xiii., and again in Books xv. and xvi., after the tremendous battle of the

Thames, when the army of Claudius was opposed in its march to Verulam, and, finally, at Camulodunum, we meet with this contingent:

> When swart Belerians, on blue Briton's part ...

> Who midst moon-shielded swart Belerians rides
> Is Decit. ...

> Halts swart Belerian king, lo, on his spear ...

> Therefore have swart Belerians crowned his brow
> With holy misselden.

This is odd in one to whom the Celts were a tall, fair-skinned, god-like people, and who, worshipping their memory, abhors and hurls curses at all the nations and races of the earth that were at enmity with them, from the conquering Romans back even to the little fierce, shrill, brown-skinned Iberians, "greedy as hawks," who had the temerity to oppose them even as in our own day the little yellow Japanese opposed the white and god-like Muscovites. For to his mind the events he relates are true, and the mighty men he brings before us, from Brennus to Caractacus, as real as any Beduin he hobnobbed with in Arabia Deserta. Perhaps it is even odder, with regard to this epic, which is undoubtedly the greatest piece of literature the young century has produced, that it should be the work of an Irishman, and from beginning to end a glorification of the Celts, yet wholly and intensely Saxon in its character, with no trace of that special quality which distinguishes the Celtic imagination.

To return. The speech of the Cornish people is another subject about which erroneous ideas may be got from reading. Norden wrote that the native language was declining in his day, and adds: "But of late the Cornishe men have much conformed themselves to the use of the Englishe toung and their Englishe is equall to the beste." There is no doubt that he was speaking of the gentry, but hasty makers of books who came after him took it to mean that the people generally spoke good English, and this statement has been repeated in books down to the present day. Andrew Borde, in his *Boke of the Introduction of Knoledge*, 1542, wrote: "In Cornwall is two speeches, the one is naughty Englische, and the other Cornysshe speeche." The last has been long dead, and dead will remain in spite of the efforts of one enthusiast who hopes to revive it and has actually written a sonnet in Cornish just to prove that it can be done but "naughty Englische" is still generally spoke, though very much less naughty than the "proper Cornish" which I have described as quite unintelligible to a stranger.

It was explained to me by a gentleman, resident for many years in West Cornwall, a student of the people, that they have two distinct ways of speaking, especially in the villages along the coast and in places much frequented by visitors. In speaking to strangers they enunciate their words with deliberation so as to be understood, and those among them who have a good deal of practice succeed very well; but among themselves they speak in a hurried manner, slurring over or omitting half the syllables in half the words, so that it is most difficult to follow them. I am convinced from my own observation that he is right. I have sat conversing with a knot of fishermen, and after a while become silent, pretending to fall into a brown study while listening all the time, and they, seeing me absorbed in my own thoughts, as they imagined, have dropped quite naturally into their own familiar lingo.

Here is another instance. There was one cottage I always liked to visit to sit for an hour with the family and sometimes have a meal with them just for the pleasure of listening to the wife, a thin, active, voluble woman, who was a remarkably good speaker, and what was even more to me, a lover of all wild creatures—a rare thing in a Cornish peasant. Or perhaps I should say all creatures save one—the adder. Once, she told me, when she was a little girl she was running home over the furze-grown hill from school when she came upon an adder in the act of devouring a nestful of fledglings. She stood still and gazed, horror-stricken, as it slowly bolted bird after bird; and then fled home crying with grief and pain at what she had witnessed, and never from that day had she seen or thought of an adder without shuddering. Now it almost invariably happened that in relating her experiences she would become excited at the most interesting part, and in her heat speak more and more rapidly and change from plain understandable English to "naughty English" or "proper Cornish," and so cause me to lose the very point, of the story. Tonkin, the Cornish historian, when the old language was well-nigh dead, described the people's speech as a jargon "the peculiarity of which was a striking uncertainty of the speaker as to where one word left off and another began."

The voice is not musical, but in young people who have not lost the quiet low manner of speaking acquired at school and gone back to the original noisy gabble, it often sounds pleasant. There is an intonation, or sing-song, which varies slightly in different localities: some fine ears can tell you to which village or "church - town," as they say, a man belongs by his intonation. As a rule it is a slight raising of the voice at the last, and dwelling on it, and on any word in the sentence on which the emphasis naturally falls, and is like singing. When you get young people with fresh, clear voices talking together with animation, the speech falls into a kind of recitative and has a rather pleasing effect. But the voice appears to harden and grow harsh with years, and acquires a disagreeable metallic quality. A good singer is, I imagine, a great rarity. The loud and hearty singing in the chapels is rather distressing. In a Bible Christian place of worship, when Baring-Gould's hymn "Onward, Christian soldiers," was being sung, I was almost deafened by the way in which the congregation bellowed out the lines—

> Hell's foundations tremble
> At our shout of praise.

And small wonder, I thought, if any sense of harmony survives down there!

Of speaking and singing I heard more than enough during my first winter (1905–6), as it was a time of political agitation. The excitement was, however, mostly in the towns. Fishermen and miners were almost to a man on the Liberal side, led by their ministers, who were eagerly looking to have their revenge on the Church; while those on the land were, despite their Methodism, on the other side, but with small hopes of winning. They appeared to be in a reticent and somewhat sullen humour: it was hard to get a word out of them, but I one day succeeded with a farmer I was slightly acquainted with. I found him in a field mending a gate, and after telling him the news and guessing what his politics were, I teased him with little mocking remarks about the way things electoral were going, until he was thoroughly aroused, and burst out in a manner that fairly astonished me. Yes, he was a Conservative, he angrily exclaimed. Being on the land, what else could he be? Only a blind fool or a traitor to his fellows could be anything different if he got his living from the land. He didn't know the man as thought different to he. But they—the farmers—were going to be beat, he knew well enough. 'Twas bound to be, seeing the other side had the numbers. They had the town people—small tradesmen, fishers, workmen and all them that passed their time leaning against a wall with their hands in their pockets—the unemployed as they was called now-days. We didn't use to call them *that*!

The Liberals with their promises had got them on their side. What did they think they'd get? To live without work? That pay would be better, clothes and food cheaper—miners to get two pounds a week, Or three, 'stead of thirty shillings; a fisherman to get twice as much for his fish, so that after a good catch he'd be able to sit down and rest for six months? No more work for we! Yes, many expected that. Anyhow they'd all git something because 'twas promised 'em—better pay, better times. But you can't have something for nothing, can you? Who's to pay for it then? They don't bother about that; 'twill have to come somehow—maybe from the land. Yes, the land's to pay for everything! Did any of them town idlers, them that worked a day or two once a week or month—did they knaw what the land gave? Did they knaw what 'tis to git up before dawn every day, Sundays as well, and work all day till after dark, all just for a bare living? But you work the land, they'll say, you don't own it—'tis the landlords we've got to get it out of. 'Twill come out of the profits. Will it? That's just what I'd like to knaw. We pay a pound or two an acre with all the rough and stones, and we pay tithes. And what do the landlords git? There's rich and poor and big and little among 'em, the same as in everything. If he owns a hundred thousand acres he's well off, however little the land pays. But what if he owns only a few small farms, like most of them in these parts—can he live and bring up his sons to be anything better than labourers, or just what we farmers are, out of it? If I owned this land myself and had to pay all my landlord pays, I don't think I'd be much better off than I am now. I'd have to work the same. What do they mean, then, by saying the land will pay? I knaw—I'll tell you. It means that the land's here and can't be hidden and can't be taken out of the country, and them who own it and them that make their living out of it can be robbed better than anybody else. That's how them that are not on the land will get their something for nothing.

What most interested me was the manner in which this discourse was delivered. In conversation he had the hard metallic Cornish voice without any perceptible intonation; now in his excitement he fell into something like a chant, keeping time with hands and legs, swinging his arms, striking his foot on the ground, and jerking his whole body up and down. Even so might some Cornish warrior of the ancient days have harangued his followers and tried to inspire in them a fury equal to his own. Even the cows two or three fields away raised their heads and gazed in our direction, wondering what the shouting was about.

As for the matter of his discourse, he expressed the feeling common among the farming people—the fear of change was on them. The odd thing is that the people generally, including miners, fishermen and others of their class, are haters of innovation, even as the farmers are, which does not promise them some material benefit, and there is no doubt that in this case they did confidently expect some good thing, and it pleased them to think their ministers were on their side. They knew that their ministers were aiming at something which they cared very little about: it was an alliance and nothing more. They are not dominated by their ministers, and, excepting some of the local preachers, do not share their malignant hatred of the Church. On the contrary, I found it a usual thing for the chapel people to go occasionally to church as well, and many made it a practice to go every Sunday to the evening service. It is also common for the chapel-goers to send for the vicar when in want of spiritual aid. The minister often enough tells the applicant to go to the vicar who is "paid to do it." I talked to scores of people about the education question and could hardly find one in ten to manifest the slightest interest in it. The people had no quarrel with the Church on that question, although their ministers were preaching to them every Sunday about it. These preachers were Scotchmen, Midlanders, Londoners—anything but Cornishmen— and in most cases knew as much about the Cornish as they did of the inhabitants of Mars. They knew what the Methodist Society wanted and that was enough for them.

Now I cared little about all this political pother. While I listened and could not avoid listening, I was like one who hears a military band with loud braying of brass instruments and rub-a-dub of drums, but is at the same time giving an attentive ear to some small sound issuing from some leafy hiding-place in the vicinity—the delicate small warble of a willow-wren, let us say. And the willow-wren in this case was the real heart of the people, not all this imported artificial noise in the air. That alone was what interested me; it was a relief to escape from the ridiculous hubbub into one of the small farm-houses, to live with the people in a house that never saw a newspaper, where the farmer and his wife minded their farm and were very proud of getting the highest price in the market for their butter.

Life on these small farms is incredibly rough. One may guess what it is like from the outward aspect of such places. Each, it is true, has its own individual character, but they are all pretty much alike in their dreary, naked and almost squalid appearance. Each, too, has its own ancient Cornish name, some of these very fine or very pretty, but you are tempted to rename them in your own mind Desolation Farm, Dreary Farm, Stony Farm, Bleak Farm, and Hungry Farm. The farm-house is a small low place and invariably built of granite, with no garden or bush or flower about it. The one I stayed at was a couple of centuries old, but no one had ever thought of growing anything, even a marigold, to soften its bare harsh aspect. The house itself could hardly be distinguished from the outhouses clustered round it. Several times on coming back to the house in a hurry and not exercising proper care I found I had made for the wrong door and got into the cow-house, or pig-house, or a shed of some sort, instead of into the human habitation. The cows and other animals were all about and you came through deep mud into the living-room. The pigs and fowls did not come in, but were otherwise free to go where they liked. The rooms were very low; my hair, when I stood erect, just brushed the beams; but the living-room or kitchen was spacious for so small a house, and had the wide old open fireplace still common in this part of the country. Any other form of fireplace would not be suitable when the fuel, consists of furze and turf.

Here I had the feeling of being back in one of those primitive cattle-breeding establishments, or *estancias* as they are called, on the South American pampas, where everyone, dogs and cats included, lived in the big smoke-blackened kitchen by day, and the fuel was dried stalks of cardoon thistle and various other stout annuals, with dried cow dung for peat, and greasy strong-smelling bones of dead horses, cows and sheep. It was like an illusion, so that I was continually on the point of addressing the children playing on the floor in Spanish, or in gaucho lingo, to name every dog "Pechicho" and call "Mees-mees" instead of "Pussy-pussy" to a cat.

By day I was out of doors, wet or fine, but in the evening—and it was when evenings were longest—I sat with the others and gazed into the cavernous fireplace and basked and shivered in the alternating bursts of heat and cold. As a rule, the round baking- pot was on its polished stone on the hearth, with smouldering turves built up round it and heaped on the flat lid. In some parts of Cornwall they have good peat, called "'pudding turves," which makes a hot and comparatively lasting fire. In the Land's End district they have only the turf taken from the surface, which makes the poorest of all fires, but it has to serve. By-and-by the big home-made loaf would be done, and when taken out would fill the room with its wholesome smell—one is almost tempted to call it fragrance. But to make a blaze and get any warmth furze was burnt. On the floor at one side of the hearth there was always a huge pile of it; the trouble was that it burnt up too quickly and took one person's whole time to keep the fire going. This onerous task was usually performed by the farmer's wife, who, after an exceedingly busy day beginning at five o'clock in the morning, appeared to regard it as a kind of rest or recreation. Standing between the hearth and pile she would pick up the top branch, and if too big with all its load of dry spines she would divide it, using her naked hands, and fling a portion on to the hearth. In a few moments the dry stuff would ignite and burn with a tremendous hissing and crackling, the flames springing up to a height of seven or eight feet in the vast hollow chimney. For a minute or two the whole big room would be almost too hot and lit up as by a flash of lightning. Then the roaring flames would sink and vanish, leaving nothing but a bed of grey ashes, jewelled with innumerable crimson and yellow sparks, rapidly diminishing. Then I would begin to think that "sitting by the fire" in this land was a mockery, that I was not warmed and made happy like a serpent in the sun, but was overcome from time to time by gusts of intolerable heat and light, with intervals of gloom that was almost darkness and bitter cold between. I should not have cared to spend the entire bitterly-cold winter of 1906–7 with no better fuel, but for a time I liked it well enough; it was a pleasure to feel the stirring to life of old instincts, to recover the associations which fire has for one that has lived in rude lands; and then, too, the glorious effect of the blaze at its greatest was intensified by the cold and gloom that preceded and followed it.

As I wished to know how they lived I had the ordinary fare and found it quite good enough for any healthy person: pork fattened on milk and home-cured; milk (from the cow) and Cornish clotted cream, which is unrivalled; sometimes a pasty, in which a little chopped-up meat is mixed with sliced turnip and onion and baked in a crust, and finally the thin Cornish broth with sliced swedes which give it a sweetish taste. Then there was the very excellent home-made bread, and saffron cake, on which the Cornish child is weaned and which he goes on eating until the last day of his life. With every meal they drink tea. They are very good eaters: one day the farmer's wife told me that each one of her six little children consumed just double what I did. And the result of this abundance and of an open-air life in that wet and windy country is that the people are as healthy and strong and long-lived as any in the world.

The children are wonderful. You may go to village after village and look in vain for a sickly or unhappy face among them. It is true you do not find the very beautiful children one often sees in both England and Ireland, the angelic children with shining golden hair, eyes of violet or pure forget-me-not blue and exquisite flesh tints, nor do you find children with so much charm. They are, generally speaking, more commonplace; the wonder is in their uniform high state of well-being.

One of the prettiest scenes I ever beheld was a procession on Empire Day, May 24, of all the school children in Penzance. They were all, even to the poorest, prettily dressed, and those of a good number of schools, Catholic, Methodist and Anglican, had very beautiful distinctive costumes. As I watched the mile-long procession going by in Market Jew Street, every face aglow with happy excitement, I began to search in the ranks for one that was thin and sad-looking or pale or anaemic but failed to find such a one.

We have been told by an English traveller in Japan that children are best off in that land where a mother is never seen to slap or heard to scold her child, and where a child is never heard to cry. Now a Japanese visitor to England has informed us that it is not so, that mothers do sometimes slap or scold a child, and children do sometimes cry. I can say the same of West Cornwall, and nevertheless believe that compared with other parts of England it is a children's paradise. A common complaint made by English residents is that the children are not taught to know their place—that they do just what they like. "When my children want to go anywhere," a mother said to me, "they do not ask my permission: but they are very good—they always tell me where they are going. I do not forbid them because I know they would go just the same." The schoolmaster in a village I stayed at told me, as an instance of the power the children have, that one morning on passing a cottage he heard sounds of crying and voices in loud argument and went in to ascertain the cause. He found the man and his wife and their two little children—Billy the boy and Winnie the girl, aged nine—all in great distress.

The man had received a letter from his cousin in Constantine to say that the village festival was about to take place and inviting him to go to him on a two or three days' visit and to take Billy. He wanted to go, and so, of course, did Billy, and now Winnie had said that she must be taken too! In vain they had reasoned with her, pointing out that she could not go because she had not been included in the invitation; she simply said that if Billy went she would go, and from that position they could not move her. The result was that the visit to Constantine had to be abandoned; the good man sadly informed the schoolmaster a day or two later that Winnie had refused to let them go without her! The odd thing, my informant said, was that there was no attempt on the parents' part to put the child down. The children, he said, are masters of the situation in these parts: the way they lorded it over their parents had amazed him when he first came from a Midland district to live among them.

But I must say for the little ones that they do not as a rule abuse their authority. They are so healthy, and have such happy and affectionate dispositions, that they do behave very well. Winnie was an exceptionally naughty little maid and required some such drastic method as that which Solomon advocated, but for the generality the system in favour is after all the one best suited to them.

AN IMPRESSION OF PENZANCE

PLACES are like faces—a first sight is almost invariably the one that tells you most. When the first sharp, clear impression has grown blurred, or is half-forgotten or overlaid with subsequent impressions, we have as a rule lost more than we have gained: it is hardly too much to say in a majority of instances that the more familiar a place becomes to us the less well we know it. At all events we have ceased to know it in the same way; we no longer vividly, consciously see it in its distinctive character.

Here it must be explained that by "place" several things are meant—the appearance of the buildings, if it be a town or village; its scenery and physical conditions generally; and, finally, its inhabitants, their physique, dress, speech and character.

Now that I know Penzance fairly well, having visited it a dozen or twenty times, occasionally staying a week or longer in it, I am glad to be able to go back to my very first impression, which, fortunately, I did not leave wholly to memory. The first visit was on a Tuesday, which is market day in Penzance, always the best day on which to visit a country town if one is interested in the people and their domestic animals. Although in midwinter, the day was exceptionally mild and very fine, and arriving early, I spent some hours in strolling about the streets, peeping into the churches, and visiting the public gardens, the sea-front and cattle-market. The town itself, despite its fine situation on Mount's Bay, with the famous castle on the island hill, opposite Marazion, on one hand, and the bold coast scenery by Newlyn and Mousehole on the other, interested me as little as any country town I have seen. Streets narrow and others narrower still, some straight, some very crooked, with houses on either side, mostly modern, all more or less mean or commonplace in appearance. The market, too, was curiously mean, and the animals poor; it was a surprise to see such cattle in a district which is chiefly dependent on dairy produce. The cows were small, mostly lean and all in an incredibly rough and dirty condition, their haunches, and in many instances half their coats, covered with an old crust of indurated mud and dung. The farmers do nothing to improve their cattle and are not only satisfied to go on keeping these small beasts of no particular breed—a red and white animal which looks like a degenerated Jersey—but it is customary to allow them to breed a year too soon.

This, however, is not a question to dogmatise about; one would certainly wish to see the beasts better cared for in the winter months and brought to market in a less filthy state, but I doubt that any improved breed would flourish in the conditions in which these animals exist in the small dairy farms on the stony moors in this rough unsheltered district. The cow of the Land's End country is, in some degree, a product of the place and in harmony with its environment, like the Land's End fox and badger.

At noon the market was over, but the town continued full of people until long after dark, the main thoroughfare, Market Jew Street, and one or two streets adjoining, being thronged with farmer folk and people from the villages who had come in to sell their produce and do their shopping. Carriers' carts stood in rows by the side of the pavements, and as in other market towns each had brought in its little cargo of humanity, mostly women with sun-browned faces, all in that rusty respectable dowdy black dress which is universal in rural England and would make an ugly object of any woman in the world. Again, as is the custom in market towns, the thoroughfare was the place where the people congregated to meet and converse with their friends and relations. This meeting with friends appeared to be a principal object of a visit to Penzance on market day. It was a sort of social function, and the longer I remained in the Street, sauntering about, watching the people and listening to endless dialogues, the more I was interested. Not only was this the healthiest-looking crowd I had ever seen in a town, without a sickly or degraded face in it, but it was undoubtedly the most cheerful, and at the same time the most sober. The liveliness of the crowd, its perpetual flow of hilarious talk, its meetings and greetings and handshakings, and its numerous little groups in eager good-humoured discussion, made me very watchful, but down to the end I was unable to detect the slightest sign of inebriety. It was a new and curious experience to find myself in a considerable gathering of rustics who had succeeded in getting through their day away from home so pleasantly without the aid of intoxicants.

Some of the town police I conversed with on the subject during the day assured me there was very little drinking going on; and that on the last occasion of the great annual fair of Corpus Christi, which lasts two or three days, when the people of all the country round are gathered in Penzance and a good deal of merry-making goes on, they had not a single case of drunkenness. The policemen, abstainers themselves they informed me, believed the people were sober because they were mostly church- and chapel-goers and had been brought up to regard intemperance as a great defect in a man and a great sin.

This explanation of the soberness of the Cornish people, especially in the west part, is, I found, the usual one: it is short and easy to carry about in the brain, and a policeman or anyone you question on the point is as ready to supply you with it as he would be to give you a match to light your pipe. Religion may be one cause, but I imagine that another and a much more important one is to be traced in the character of this people.

I here recall a striking explanation of the drinking habit in England given me by an independent witness and a very keen observer. He was an Argentine of an old native family. I first knew him as a young student; he rose afterwards to a very high place in the government of his country, and a few years ago, while on a visit to England, he looked me up and we renewed our old friendship.

His idea about drinking in England was that it was indulged in to remedy a defect in us, a certain slowness or dullness of thought or feeling from which we desired at times to escape. He gave the following illustration. Two British workmen, old friends, meet by chance after a long interval and clasp hands delightedly and each asks the other how he is. One says "Just so-so" or "Pretty well," the other says "Mustn't grumble." They appear, then, to have got to the end of their powers of speech, yet are conscious that there is more to be said if they are ever to get back into the old comfortable intimacy. Suddenly one has an inspiration and proposes a drink. The other agrees with a sense of relief, and they incontinently repair to the nearest public, where, after a glass or two, what they desired and tried to get but could not is at once theirs: their tongues are loosed, they laugh in pure joy at their new-found freedom and ability to express themselves; they talk of their work, their families, of a hundred things they had forgotten but remember now, and are glad to feel in sympathy with each other.

Now, he continued, we of another race and disposition in our country when we meet an old friend, although it may not be very long since we last saw him, feel no such restraint, but at once the joy of meeting him sets us off. The pleasure is stimulus enough of itself; it sends the blood spinning through our brains, and we are, in fact, almost intoxicated by it. To take alcohol is unnecessary, and would, indeed, be very foolish.

So far my Argentine friend, and whether he was right or wrong it struck me at Penzance that the naturally lively disposition of Cornishmen, their quick feeling and responsiveness, was the chief cause of their temperance in drink. This made it easy for them to practise temperance; it made it possible for friend to meet friend and spend the day without an artificial aid to cheerfulness.

It is true that the Irish, racially related to the Cornish and resembling them in disposition, are not a sober people; on this point I will only venture to suggest that their love of whisky and ether may not result from the same cause as the Anglo-Saxon's love of drink. Probably their misery has got a great deal to do with it, for just as whisky or beer will unfreeze the currents of the soul in two stolid English friends and set them flowing merrily, so in men of all races will alcohol lift them above themselves and give them a brief happiness.

It may seem odd to quote the Rev. R. J. Campbell in this connection, but I find in a recent pronouncement of his a curiously apposite remark about drunkenness. "The man," he says, "who got dead drunk last night did so because of the inspiration in him to break through the barriers of his limitations, to express himself and realise the more abundant life." We need not follow him any further in his quaint contention that sin is, after all, nothing but a spasmodic effort of the sinner to reach to or capture higher things—a "quest of God" as he curiously puts it. It is nothing but a prolonged and somewhat shrill echo of a wiser or a saner man's thoughts. "The sway of alcohol over mankind," says Professor William James in his *Varieties of Religious Experience*, "is unquestionably due to its power to stimulate the mystical faculties of human nature, usually crushed to earth by the cold facts and dry criticisms of the sober hour. Sobriety diminishes, discriminates and says, No; drunkenness expands, unites and says, Yes . . . It brings its votary from the chill periphery of things to the radiant core. It makes him for the moment one with truth . . . it is part of the deeper mystery and tragedy of life that whiffs and gleams of something that we immediately recognise as excellent should be vouchsafed to so many of us only in the fleeting earlier phases of what in its totality is so degrading a poisoning."

Mr. Campbell's striver after the higher life who got dead drunk last night is brother to the savage. It is stated by no less an authority on the drink question than Dr. Archdall Reid that there is in man a passion, an instinct, for alcohol, and that the savage has a craving for drink. There is no such craving. The natural happiness of the savage, as I know him, is in hunting and fighting; and in the intervals of those stirring pursuits he has a somewhat dull, lethargic existence. Alcohol produces the state of mind he is in when occupied with the chase or in raiding and fighting. It is a joyful excitement, a short cut to happiness and glory which he will take at every opportunity. They will even sell their weapons and the skins that cover them for a little of this happiness; but when there is no more of it to be had they return to their normal life, and think no more about it unless the poison has permanently or very seriously injured them. One effect on the poisoned man, savage or civilised, is that "craving," or mad thirst, with which, Dr. Reid imagines, Nature has cursed her human children.

We have now got a good distance away from the subject we started with; but I have no intention of returning to Penzance. That town interested me solely as a place where Cornishmen may be seen and studied. To go back a little further in time to my first impressions of Cornwall, I was struck, as most persons are on a first visit, with its unlikeness to other parts of England. You find the unlikeness not only in the aspect of the country, but in the people too; you would hardly feel that you had gone so far from the England you know if you had crossed the Atlantic. The differences are many and great, but in this chapter I am concerned with only one—the greater temperance of the people: indeed, my impression of Penzance was given mainly to serve as an introduction to this subject. It is a very important one. Our judges and magistrates are always telling us that most of the crimes committed in this country are due to drink. The case of Cornwall certainly favours that view: it is, if the statistics are accepted as showing the true state of things, the most sober and has the cleanest record in the land. The Devonians are not a vicious people; they compare well enough with most counties, and they are next-door neighbours to the Cornish; yet the indictable offences in Devon are about double per thou sand of the population to those of Cornwall. What is the reason of this? Why are the Cornish more temperate than others?

I am sorry I ever wasted an hour over a book on Cornwall with the idea that it would be helpful to me. The time would have been more profitably spent if I had stood with my hands in my pockets watching a sparrow carry up straws to its nesting- hole under the eaves; or better still, if I had talked to a child or an old man in some village street. To read is to imbibe false ideas, and in the end, if you are capable of observing for yourself and care anything about the matter, you are put to the trouble of ridding yourself of them.

When the Penzance policemen—abstainers and religious men themselves—gave me a reason for the people's soberness they were telling me what they had been taught, and I accepted it as probably true. I too had read that statement and here was a confirmation of it! It is a great satisfaction, a relief, to have our problems solved for us. Blessings on the man who runs out before us to remove some obstacle from the path!

But the relief was not for long: doubts began to assail me. What the good policeman had said was what the Methodists have been saying in their writings these hundred years or longer: they are saying it now, all the time, and believe it because it flatters them, and poor weak humanity is ever credulous of a flattering falsehood.

One day, a few miles from Penzance, I met a young coastguardsman and had a nice long talk with him, in the course of which he gave me his impression of the country. For he was not a native and had not long been in Cornwall; he came from South Wales where he had been stationed two or three years. The people of that place—I will not mention the locality—were, he said, horrible to live with, degraded and brutish beyond what he could have imagined possible in any civilised country. They were drunkards, fighters, dreadfully profane, and as to lechery— called immorality in the journals and blue-books—no woman could go out after dark, or by day into any lonely place, without danger of assault. The change to West Cornwall was so great that for several weeks he could not realise it; he could not believe that the people were all sober and decent and friendly in disposition as he had been assured. When he spied a man coming along the road his impulse was to lower his eyes or turn his face away to avoid seeing a brutalised countenance. He always expected to hear some obscene expression or a torrent of profanity from every stranger he met. Even now, after some months in this new clean land, he had not grown quite accustomed to regard everyone, stranger or not, as a being just like himself, one he could freely address and feel sure of receiving friendly pleasant words in return.

It was interesting to hear the coastguardsman's story because of his feelings in the matter and what the change to Cornwall meant to him. That he was right in his facts we know. We know, for instance, that just as Cornwall is the cleanest county, so some of the Welsh counties— especially in the coal-mining districts—are the foulest. Yet the Welsh are Celts too and Methodists of a hundred and fifty years' standing! They are, in fact, the truer Methodists if we consider what that creed is and that its most essential point is that there can be no salvation without a sudden conversion, with or without the accompaniment of groanings, shriekings, and other manifestations of the kind. But what are the facts of the case as to the condition of Cornwall, with regard to drunkenness, before its conversion to Methodism? They are not so easily got as one may think. There is plenty of material, and any one with a preconceived opinion on the question would doubtless find something to confirm him in it. I had no opinion, and my sole desire was to find out the truth. My first superficial study of the question made me a believer in the claim made by the Methodists, but it did not bear a closer investigation. What I found was that when tin-mining was in a highly prosperous state and the population of the mining centres vastly greater than it is now, there was a good deal of intemperance among the miners; but there is nothing to show that they were as degraded as the Welsh of to-day. It is also indisputable that Wesley's preaching had a profound effect on the tin-miners. That is the most that can be said. That the Methodism invented after Wesley's death and imposed on his followers in his name—the name of one who abhorred Dissent—is the cause of the temperance of the Cornish people generally there is no evidence to show, and no reason to believe. On the contrary there is very good reason for disbelief.

The Cornish people are incomparably better off now, so far as material comforts go, than they were in the last half of the sixteenth century, when Richard Carew wrote his *Survey of Cornwall*; but there have been no really great, no radical changes—no transformations, as in so many other parts of Britain. The life of to-day is very much like the old life, and the people now are like their forefathers of three centuries ago as described by Carew. He pointed out that the tin-mines were a great evil—the curse of Cornwall, since it was impossible for the miners to escape the abominable temptations to drink which were thrust in their way. Every second house was a drinking-place, into which the poor wretches were enticed to waste their earnings, with the result that their families were in a chronic state of want. But rural population were in a very different case; those who worked on the land were indeed poor, fared coarsely, dressed meanly and wore no shoes, but they were sober and industrious and lived in decent homes, and their wives and children were properly fed and clothed; so that in the end they were far better off and happier than the workers in the mines.

So we arrive at the conclusion that the Cornish people are not, and never have been, intemperate generally; for one reason, because they are of a singularly happy disposition, lively and sociable, with a very intense love of their families and homes; and secondly, because of the idyllic conditions in which they exist, and always have existed, in a country thinly populated, without big towns, with the healthiest, most equable and genial climate in Britain; and, best of all, isolated, outside of and remote from civilisation with its feverish restlessness, vices and dreadful problems.

MANNERS AND MORALS

"AFTER having marched over the land, and waded through the sea, to describe all the creatures therein, insensible and sensible, the course of method summoneth me to discourse of the reasonable, to wit, the inhabitants."

Thus said Richard Carew in his *Survey of Cornwall*, written at the end of the sixteenth century. I have no course of method, nor any order in which to record these impressions of rocks and waters and birds and flowers, or any other thing, insensible or sensible; but now, after having written one entire long chapter on the soberness of the Cornish people, explaining the causes, as I conceive them, of this peculiar state, I think it may be just as well to go on about the reasonable, to wit the inhabitants, and endeavour to get a little nearer to a proper understanding of them. And here I must modify what I said in my haste about the worthlessness (to me) of all books on Cornwall, protesting that my time would have been better spent in listening to the chirruping of a cock sparrow than in reading them. Carew's book is a notable exception, pleasant and profitable to read after three centuries, and, if we exclude living authors, it may be described as the one very good book ever written by a Cornishman.

Having said so much it strikes me as an odd fact that the boast Carew made about his important and long-living book—that it was his very own, or, to use his more picturesque expression, that he gathered the sticks for the building of his poor nest—I, too, can make of this unimportant work which may not have more years of life than the *Survey* has had centuries.

For impressions of nature one goes to nature—the visible world which lies open before us; but when it comes to that other nature of the human heart, half-hidden in clouds and mist and half-revealed in gleams of the

sun, one modestly looks to others for guidance and to the books which
have been written in the past. And of books there are plenty—histories,
topographies, guides, hand-books, tours, travels, itineraries, journeys and
journals, wherein are many useful facts originally collected very long
ago and carried on from book to book—facts about the pilchard fishery,
tin and tin-mining, geology and natural history, Cornish crosses and
cromlechs with other antiquities; also legends of saints and giants and the
happenings of a thousand years ago. But about the reasonable, to wit the
inhabitants, next to nothing, and that very little as a rule misleading. It is
mostly of a flattering description.

It is indeed curious to note that while those who have written on the
Cornish people almost invariably say the pleasantest things about them,
the English, or Anglo-Saxons, who live among them, the strangers who
reside permanently or for long periods within their gates, have a very
different opinion. The praise and the dispraise to my mind are equally far
from the truth; moreover, it is not difficult to discover the reason of such
widely divergent opinions. Those who visit the land to write a book about
it, or for some other purpose, but do not remain long enough to know
anything properly, are charmed and misled by the exceedingly friendly and
pleasant demeanour towards strangers which is almost universal, seeing
in it only the outward expression of divers delightful qualities. Those
who live with the people, if they happen to be Saxons, discover that the
friendliness is a manner, that when you penetrate beneath it you come
upon a character wholly un-Saxon, therefore of a wrong description or
an inferior quality. For it is a fact that the Englishman is endowed with a
very great idea of himself, of the absolute rightness of his philosophy of
life, his instincts, prepossessions, and the peculiar shape and shade of his
morality. He is, so to speak, his own standard, and measures everybody
from China to Peru by it, and those who fall short of it, who have a
somewhat different code or ideal, are of the meaner sort of men which
one expects to find outside of these islands. It is undoubtedly a noble
state of mind, befitting a world-conquering people, and has served to
make us respected, feared and even disliked in other countries, but some
small disadvantages and some friction result from it at home, and one is
that the lord of human kind residing among inferior Celts finds himself
out of harmony with the people about him. He is not as a rule quick, but
after a few months or years in a place he begins to find his neighbours
out, and they on their side are not insensible of the change in his regard.
He sees that they have faults and vices which, being unlike those of the
English, he finds it hard to tolerate. Not only does he disapprove of them

on this account, but he resents having been taken in. "You are charmed with this people, you tell me! Wait till you have lived years with them as I have done and know them as I do, then give me your opinion," they are accustomed to say in their bitterness—the feeling which cannot but make a man unjust.

It is not easy or not pleasant to descend to particulars, but having gone so far as to state the question it would hardly be fair not to go further, although by so doing I shall most probably incur the displeasure of both sides.

A common charge against the Cornish is a want of solidity or stability of character. You cannot rely on them. You are constantly deceived by their manner: they the readiest of any people on earth to fall in with your views and do exactly what you want. *But they don't do it.* You may waste years or indeed your whole life in striving to make them see things in your better way, and give them every instruction and make them understand (for they are not stupid) how much more may be done by following an improved method, and you will always be brought back to the same old *We don't belong to do it that way*, and after a hundred or a thousand trials you give it up in despair. Or you may take your defeat philosophically (with a little added wormwood) and say that although they are not stupid, their intelligence, like that of the lower animals, is non-progressive.

Then as to the one-and-all spirit. This, I am assured on all hands, is the veriest fiction, or at all events it is quite a different thing from what it is usually supposed to be. The members of each little community are as a fact more unfriendly and spiteful towards one another than is the case in an English village: they are *one* only when they make a combined attack on some person who has been so unfortunate as to offend everybody at the same time. So envious are they that everyone hates to see any benefit or gift bestowed on another. You must treat all alike; you may not give a hundred of coals to the poorest, most suffering old woman without exciting general ill-will, unless you are prepared to give as much to every other old woman in the parish. They would rather the old creature should be left to shiver in a fireless room. Nor must you speak in praise of another: do not say to Mrs. Trevenna, what a nice, or what a well-behaved, or pretty, or attractive child that is of your sister or friend or neighbour, Mrs. Trevasgis, if you do not want to set the Trevenna tongue wagging against both you and the Trevasgis woman.

These little uncharitablenesses to describe them all in one word—are universal in man or woman, perhaps in both, and being part of our nature they probably have their uses: if they strike us more in the Cornish than in our own people it is because of the difference of temperament or disposition—because their feelings, good or bad, are more readily excited and are expressed with less restraint.

That they are not truthful and not honest is another count in the long indictment. With regard to honesty it is one I always hear with surprise; for can it be said that we are as a people honest? Consider the one matter of our food and drink—the amount of legislation we have found necessary on the subject, the cost to the country of maintaining a vast army of inspectors and analysts to prevent us from poisoning each other for the sake of a small extra gain! Would anyone in England give me for love or money a glass of milk or beer, or a slice of bread and butter, which would not seriously injure my health but for the fear of the law? And after all we have done to protect ourselves we are assured every day by the experts that we are living in a fool's paradise, seeing that dishonesty is so ingrained in us that it will always find out a way to defeat our best efforts.

This charge may then be dropped—for the present at all events. When our moral condition has been properly examined and reported on by travellers and missionaries from Thibet or some undiscovered country on the other side of the Mountains of the Moon, we may be in a position to affirm that Cornwall is not as honest as, say, Middlesex.

But if honesty is or ought to be a painful subject, perhaps in discussing the question of truthfulness we shall be able to make out a better case and recover our self-esteem. Here we have it as it is stated by one of my correspondents:

> However bad the English commercial morality may be, the average Englishman's word still stands for something. When he lies he does so deliberately for some important purpose. Some other races, including the Celts, appear to have a different perception of truth, and to lie, as children do, readily and gracefully, because lies and exaggerations are more interesting and agreeable than plain truth. A difference of temperament: the Englishman may be better or worse, but he knows where he is and resents being fooled.

This reminds me of the experience of a young friend of mine, a pure Englishman, exceptionally intelligent, and so sympathetic and adaptive that he is happy with all sorts of people and they with him. From boyhood he has lived in Wales, a somewhat rambling life, in towns, villages and farm-houses, and his playmates, fellow-students and companions have been natives. Yet he assures me that he has never been able to feel himself one of them, and never been able to see anything eye to eye with even his most intimate and dearest friends of that race. It all seems to come to an ineradicable difference of mind in the two races. There is no better and no worse, and the only quarrel is when anyone, Saxon or Celt, is offended at another's inability to see eye to eye with him, regarding it as a bad habit which ought to be overcome, or a sheer piece of perversity on his part.

Then we have the complicated question of morality, or rather of "immorality," by which some journalists, authors and compilers of blue-books mean sexual intercourse unsanctified by marriage. Norden, who wrote nigh on three centuries before the nice modern mind invented a new meaning for an old word, described it as the "sweet synn" which was regarded as venial in Cornwall. But Norden spoke of the gentry; the manners and morals of what he described as the "baser sort of men," including rustics, miners, mechanics, farmers and yeomen, did not interest his lofty mind. But the sweet sin was also common among Norden's "baser sort of men," and exists to-day as it did in the past, and as it exists in the Principality, and perhaps in Ireland, where the power and vigilance of the priests are now able to keep it dark. It is really not so much a vice as a custom of the country, perhaps of the race, seeing that the illicit intercourse usually ends in marriage. It has been said that in Cornwall matrimony is the result of maternity. For it must be borne in mind that I am speaking only of Cornwall. We have seen in the last chapter how it is in Wales, in some of the mining districts; but these bestial developments are not known and have probably never existed in the duchy. It is true that some poor women are left to bear their burden alone, and that their frail sisters who have had better fortune are as ready as others to persecute them, but the proportion of these unhappy ones is really less than in very many English villages.

It is of the villages and small towns I speak: the towns are mostly very small; but as population increases with the revival of the mining industry (the curse of the country "from ancientie"), the extraordinary liberty which young women are allowed, or have taken for themselves, and their pleasant ways with men may result in a troublesome problem in the larger centres.

It is said of the Cornish, as it has been said of the Irish and of Celtic people generally, that they are cruel. I doubt if they are more cruel than others if we restrict the word to its proper meaning—the infliction of pain for the pleasure of it; but there us a great deal of barbarity of the kind one sees in Spanish and Italian countries which results from temper.

The Cornish, like the Spanish, are passionate, and when anything goes wrong they are apt to wreak their fury on the poor unresisting beast—cow, calf, horse, donkey or sheep. I have witnessed many shocking acts of this kind which it would be too painful to me to have to describe, and in discussing this subject with others, some of them Cornishmen who naturally love their people and are anxious to see them in the most favourable light, they have confessed to me that this kind of brutality is very common; that it is the greatest blot, on the Cornish man's character and a constant cause of pain to persons of a humane disposition. What to me makes it peculiarly painful is the knowledge that the man I have witnessed horribly ill-treating some patient dumb beast, and hated and wished that I had had the power to annihilate him—this very man, his fit of fury over, would prove himself a genuine Cornishman, a very pleasant fellow, temperate, religious, hospitable, a good husband, devoted to his children. Celtic cruelty, Tennyson said, was due to want of imagination. He was speaking of the Irish, who are not supposed to be without that faculty. Whether or not the Cornish have it is another question, but it may be that Celtic cruelty, like the Spanish, is due rather to a drop of black blood in the heart—an ancient latent ferocity which comes out in moments of passion.

The fact that prosecutions for cruelty to animals are so rare—one case, I should say, in about every five thousand getting into court—reminds me here of another charge brought against the Cornish by the strangers within their gates. If Cornwall, the critics say, is able to show the cleanest record in England it is because the law-breakers are not treated as in other counties. Offences are winked at or over-looked by the police in many instances, and when a prosecution takes place magistrates will not convict if they can possibly help it. Not only are they too tolerant and hate to hurt one of their own people, but they think of themselves, of their own material interests, and are anxious above all things that their county should maintain its nice reputation.

Something more will have to be said on the subject of cruelty to animals in another chapter about wild birds during severe weather. At present, to conclude this chapter, we have to consider another matter which is that of the gravest charge of all and is indicated in the following words spoken to me by a professional man, a resident in West Cornwall. "I have lived and worked for twenty years among this people and have long lost the last vestige of respect and affection I once had for them. They are at heart what their forefathers were; their religion, softer manners and apparent friendliness to strangers, is all on the surface—a veneer. The old barbarism lives and burns under it, and if it were not for the watch kept on them and the altered conditions generally, they would go gladly back to the ancient trade of wrecking."

This spontaneous outburst on the part of a person occupying an important position in the community made me curious to know more about the man himself. He was in a sense a good man, a generous giver according to his means, and as he gave secretly even those who hated him (because they knew, I imagine, that he despised and hated them) were never unwilling to go to him for help when they required it. But he was by nature an alien, one of those downright uncompromising Saxons who cannot get on with those of a different and in some things antagonistic race. He had tried his best to bridge the gulf over. His ambition had been to make himself the most loved man in the place, and naturally his signal failure had embittered him.

But what about the charge? Was there a particle of truth in it? And, finally, what is meant by *wrecking*?

I take it that two distinct things are meant—one a very black crime indeed, the other nothing worse than a disregard of regulations and petty pilfering. With regard to the first, it is believed from certain stories and traditions which have come down to us, the origin of which is lost in the mists of antiquity, that the natives of the dangerous parts of the coast made it a custom to lure vessels on to the rocks to their destruction by displaying false lights. This may be true: we know that the various races and tribes composing the nation—Celts and Saxons, Danes and Normans—vied with each other in every form of atrocity and of cruelty; but no instance of the crime in question can be authenticated as having taken place in recent times. Nevertheless the belief is cherished and kept alive in books, mainly religious tales and novels, that this frightful custom continued down to the middle of the eighteenth century when Wesley appeared to convert the Cornish people from their vicious ways and all kinds of wickedness, including that of deliberately wrecking vessels and murdering the unhappy wretches who succeeded in escaping from the fury of the waves. As the books containing these veracious statements, so flattering to the Cornish, are exceedingly popular in the duchy and nowhere out of it, the Cornish people are themselves responsible for keeping these fables alive.

As for the other lesser crime or offence, I fancy that it is not one an Englishman can look on as a very serious matter.

I was one day discussing the Sunday observance question with an English clergyman whose parish lies on the Cornish coast, and related the following incident to him. I was lodging with an intelligent and well-to-do artisan and his wife in a Somerset village when one Sunday morning, the weather being very fine, my host, finding that I was not going to church, asked me if I would take a walk with him as he wished to show me some nice spots in the neighbouring woods and copses where he was accustomed to go. The woods were certainly very beautiful, with green open spaces and a fine stream where we watched the trout and saw a kingfisher flash by. We said it was not a bad place to spend a Sunday morning in and then fell into a long talk about Sunday observance, and the fact that village people, the men especially, had lost the habit of going to church, but had discovered no way of spending the day pleasantly or profitably. I thought that outdoor games ought to be encouraged as it was plainly beneficial both to mind and body and saved them from tedium and the temptations to drink and smoke more than was good for them. I thought too that when the parson of the parish took this line the effect was entirely good; it taught them to look on him as more human and one of themselves and capable of putting himself in their place.

My companion looked grave and shook his head at this, and when I told him that I knew clergymen who were as good men as could be found in the land who agreed with my view, and were the promoters of Sunday games in their parishes, he answered that if a thing were wrong, even ministers of the Gospel could not make it right. He was in the middle of his argument when we came out from a big copse into a large open space, and created a panic in a multitude of rabbits feeding there. Away they scuttled in every direction—hundreds of rabbits, old and half-grown young. Going a little further we noticed our small spaniel sniffing at a burrow. "He's a clever little dog," said my companion; "he always lets me know when a rabbit is not too far down." With that he got down on the turf, and thrusting his arm in to the shoulder, quickly pulled out a young rabbit, which, after snapping its neck, he thrust into his large coat-tail pocket. Putting his arm down again he pulled out a second one, then a third, and having snapped their necks and pocketed them, he got up and we resumed our walk and our discussion. "No, no," he said. "I'm not a religious man, and don't go to church as a rule, but I draw the line at playing games on a Sunday."

Then he came to a stop beside a close thicket of brambles and thorn, and began pulling the rabbits out of his pocket. "After all I don't want them, and they are a nuisance to carry," he said, and with that he threw them into the thicket.

That was my story.

"We are just as consistent here," said the Cornish clergyman. "The people are religious and strict Sabbatarians; they go regularly to church or chapel, but if a vessel in distress is in sight, and there is a chance of its going on the rocks, they make an exception; they will pace the cliffs all day long in the hope of a bit of flotsam coming in their way."

They may appear equally inconsistent—the Somerset man and the Cornishman—but can we say that one is morally worse than the other? The case of the good artisan who drew the line at cricket on Sunday is not a singular one: one doubts if there is a peasant in England, however truly religious a man he may be, who would not pick up a rabbit or hare if he got the chance on any day of the week. They do not believe it is wrong, consequently it does not hurt their conscience, and the only fear they have is to be found out. And so with the Cornish man; it is ingrained in him, and is like an inherited knowledge, that if the Power that rules the winds and waves, and who holds the lives of all men in the hollow of his hand, sends a ship upon the rocks, it is because he thinks proper to destroy that ship and incidentally to scatter gifts among his people living on the coast. Shall they refuse to take any good thing he chooses to send them? If their minister tells them it is wrong it is because he does not know the rights of it. Their fathers did it, and their fore-fathers, for generations back and were no worse for it. It would indeed be strange if they did not resent as an injustice, an interference with their natural rights, that so strict a watch is kept on them, and that they are forbidden to take anything the waves may cast up in their way.

Quite recently we had some rather startling manifestations of this feeling, and one amusing instance may be given. Just after a big ship had come to grief on the rocks, at the most dangerous point on the coast, another ship was in great peril near the same spot; fortunately, towards evening the weather moderated a little and it began to look as if there was not going to be a second disaster just then. My informant was standing on the shore with some of the fishermen of the place, looking at the sea. The sky was clearing and the sun, near the horizon, came forth a great globe of red fire and threw its light over the tumultuous waters. Then all at once one of the men burst out in a storm of execration, and cursed the sun and wind and sea and pretty well the whole universe. For it seemed so hard just when things were looking so well that the sun should shine and the wind begin to fall and the sea moderate! My informant asked him indignantly how he, a Christian man, could entertain such feelings and how he dared to express them. He answered by putting out his right arm and baring it to the elbow, then, feeling the muscles with the fingers of the left hand, he said, with a somewhat rueful expression, "It's in the bone, *and we can't help it!*"

Yet this very man had been foremost in the work of rescuing the people in the ship that had gone on the rocks.

My informant happens to be one of the Englishmen in Cornwall who do not experience that antipathy or sense of separation in mind from the people they live with, and are not looked at as foreigners. I have met with several such who have very pleasant relations with their neighbours, and can love and are loved by them, and are almost able to forget that they are not natives. But, unless I am mistaken, in such cases the stranger is not wholly a stranger; in other words he is partly of the same race, therefore able to sympathise and to identify himself with them. And it may be due to the Celtic element in me that I feel very much at home with the people. A Dumnonian, if not a "swart Belerian," with an admixture of Irish blood, I feel myself related to them and therefore do not think they can justly resent my having described them as I have found them without the usual pretty little lying flatteries. Your relations are privileged critics. Moreover, if I love them they cannot, according to their own saying, have any but a kindly feeling for me. "Karenza whelas karenza" is all the Cornish I know.

CORNISH HUMOUR

IT is permissible to a writer once in a lifetime to illustrate his work by an allusion to that celebrated "Chapter on Snakes," in an island in which these reptiles are not found. But I am not saying that there is no humour in Cornwall. There may be such a thing; but if you meet with it you will find that it is of the ordinary sort, only of an inferior quality, and that there is very little. What I can say is, there is no Cornish humour, no humour of the soil and race, as there is an Irish and a Scotch humour, and even as there is an English humour, which may be of a poor description in comparison with the Hibernian, but is humour nevertheless, native and local, and not confined to Dorset and Warwickshire, but to be met with in every county from the Tamar to the Tweed.

This came as a great surprise to me since I had often read in books and articles about the country that the Cornish are a humorous folk, and those who have been there and profess to know the people say that it is so. Their humour, like their imagination (for they are also credited with that faculty), is sometimes vaguely described as of the Celtic sort. My surprise was all the greater when I came and saw the people and received confirmation, as I imagined, through the sense of sight of all I had been told. They looked it, yet were without it; the signs, "gracious as rainbows," deceived me (as they had doubtless deceived others), but only for a season; they were the outward marks of quite other pleasing qualities with which we are not now concerned. I looked for humour and met with some amusing adventures in my search for that rare, elusive quality.

Walking to a village one day I fell in with a man who had, like many a West Cornishman, a strikingly Irish countenance, also an Irish voice and flow of spirits. Hearing where I was going he at once undertook to show me the nearest way. It would, he asserted, save me a good mile: *his* way proved in the end two miles further than the one I had chosen, but it led him near to his own cottage and he wanted badly to shorten the way with talk—that was all. I did not mind, because I wished to listen to him, thinking that I had at length got hold of the right person, one who would give me a taste of the genuine native humour. Not a bit of it! He talked freely of many things—his native place, his family, his neighbours, the good and the bad in them, his past life and labours, future prospects and much more—a long talk which an Irishman would have enlivened with many flashes of quaint humour, but there was not the faintest trace of such a quality in it.

Later in the same day I walked by a footpath which led me through what is called the "town-place" of a small farm-house. Here I found two men engaged in an animated discussion, and one, in ragged clothes, with a pitchfork in his hand, was the very type of a wild Irishman; in all Connemara you would not find a more perfect specimen—rags, old battered hat, twinkling grey-blue Irish eyes, a shock of the most fiery carroty red hair, and, finally, a short black clay pipe, or dhudeen, in his mouth. Yet even this man, delightful to look at, proved when I conversed with him just as prosaic and disappointing as the other.

I certainly did not expect to find anything in these two and in scores more I had intercourse with which could be set down in a note-book as specimens of Cornish humour. One may spend days among Irish peasants and never hear anything worth repeating, especially in writing. Indeed, most of what we recognise as Irish humour is not translatable into written language. It is like the quality of charm in women, something personal which you receive directly and cannot convey to another. But you are all the time conscious of the humorous spirit in them; you see it in their eyes and mobile mouth gestures, and you catch its accent in their speech. And you feel how good a thing it is; that a people possessing this quality, or faculty, in so eminent a degree is not so poor as others who have more comforts and are more civilised; that even want and squalor, and misery, and vice, and crime, are not as ugly and disgusting as they appear among those who are with out this sparkling spirit, this lightning of the soul, with its unexpected flashes, which throws a brightness on everything.

The people of the extreme west of Cornwall have so close a resemblance to the Irish in feature and expression that quite often enough when with them, in farms and hamlets, I could hardly avoid falling into the illusion that I was in Ireland. It is this look in them, or in many of them, which makes the want of the Irishman's most engaging quality so strange and almost incredible. There is an expression of the Irish peasant's face which is exceedingly common—one could almost say that it is universal—which one comes to regard as an expression of a humorous mind. It is most marked in those who see you as a stranger among them, or in those you meet casually and converse with. It is a peculiarly shrewd penetrating look in the eyes, which appear to be examining you very narrowly while passing itself off as mere friendly interest in you; and with that look in the eye there is a lighting up of the whole face. The man, you imagine, is looking out for some signal of a sympathetic or understanding spirit in you, a token of kinship: but when we go further and imagine it a humorous spirit we are probably mistaken. We associate that peculiar expression of the eyes with the humorous mind because we have found them together in so many persons—if we have been in Ireland. In the Cornishman, too, that same expression of the eyes is exceedingly common—an expression which even more than feature makes him differ so greatly from the Anglo-Saxon. But it does not denote humour, seeing that he is inferior to the dullest of the English in this respect. But he is more alive than the Englishman, and his ever-fresh child-like curiosity makes him seem more human.

This peculiar Irish-like alertness and liveliness of mind, with a total want of a sense of humour, struck me forcibly in the case of another Cornish man I encountered in my rambles. But before I get to this story another must be told by way of introduction.

Frequently in my wanderings on foot in that stoniest part of a stony land, called the Connemara of Cornwall, where indeed the likeness of the people to the Irish is most marked, I recalled an old anecdote about a stony country which I heard in boyhood. I heard it one morning at the breakfast table in my early home in South America. We had a big party in the house, and the talk turned on the subject of sharp and clever replies made by natives to derisive questions asked by travellers. Several of the men present had been great travellers themselves, and almost everyone had a good story or two to relate, but the best of all was one of a traveller who had been walking for many hours in one of the stoniest districts he had ever been in. As far as he could see on every side the earth was strewn with masses of stone, and he was quite tired of the endless desolation. At length he came on a native engaged in piling up stones in a field, and approaching him addressed him as follows: "My good man, can you tell me where the people of these parts procure stone with which to build their houses?" That was the mocking question, and the witty answer of the native created a great laugh at the table, but unfortunately I have forgotten what it was. I have tried in that stony place to recall it without success. It may be that some reader of this chapter has heard and remembers the answer; if so, I hope he will have the goodness to communicate it to me, and relieve my tired mind from further efforts to recover it.

Now one day in Cornwall, while walking on a vast stony hill above the little village of Towednack, I spied a man at work digging up stone in the middle of a freshly ploughed field at the foot of the hill. He had a crowbar, which he would thrust down into the soil to find where there was stone near the surface; then with his three-cornered, long-handled spade he would dig down and expose it, and if too large to be lifted he would, with drill and wedges and iron mallet, split it up into pieces of a convenient size. In this way he had raised a vast heap of stones, which would be carted away by-and-by.

It came into my head to try my old story as an experiment on this man, and I went down the hill to him and after saluting him stood some time admiring his tremendous energy. He was a slim wiry man of about thirty or thirty-five, good-looking, with a Celtic face and that lively shrewd expression which one associates with the Irishman's humorous spirit. After watching him for a few minutes at his frantic task I said, "By the by, I wish you would tell me where they get the stone in this part of the country to build their houses with?"

He turned and stared me in the face with the greatest astonishment, then throwing out his hand in an angry way towards the vast heap of black wet chunks of granite he had dragged out of the earth, he cried, "This is stone! This is what they build houses with in this part of the country! Stone! granite!—there's enough of it in the ground to build all the houses we want, and *on* the ground too!"

Then he stared again and finally waved his arm towards the hill I had descended from, strewn all over with huge boulders and masses of granite, and added, "All you've got to do is to use your own eyes and they'll show you where we get stone to build houses with!"

I was obliged to explain that I had only asked that preposterous question in fun: then he calmed down and stood silent for some time, with eyes resting on a chunk of granite at his feet, revolving the matter in his mind, but he did not appear to think there was anything very funny in it. But the extraordinary thing was that after he had quite got over the uncomfortable feeling I had given him—the suspicion, perhaps, that his interlocutor was not quite right in his head—he proved as lively and agreeable a talker as I have met among the Cornish people of his class, and gave me an entertaining account of the various occupations he had followed since the tin-mine in which he had worked as a boy had been abandoned. He was, in fact, a very intelligent fellow, with nice feelings and sentiments, and as pleasant to talk with as anyone could be without a sense of humour.

When we look for something and find it not, our non-success is apt to produce a dogged spirit in us and we go on looking even after our reason has assured us that the object sought for is not there, or has no existence. That is how it was with me; I was determined to find that rarity in Cornwall—a man with a sense of humour. And in my quest I did not hold my tongue about my encounter with the stone-digger; I told it to at least a dozen persons and they one and all received it coldly. The last one was a farmer; he listened attentively, then after an interval of silence remarked, "Yes, I see; the man did not understand your question in the sense you meant. It was a joke and he took it seriously; I see."

He saw but he didn't smile, and I thereupon resolved never again to tell the story of the man digging granite in a ploughed field to anyone in Cornwall.

Another instance of this curious child-like simplicity of mind in the native was almost painful. To have one's words taken literally in some cases produces the uncomfortable feeling that there is something wrong with the brain of the person spoken to. I was walking on the moor one day in spring in oppressingly warm weather when, on passing close by a small farm-house, I caught sight of the farmer standing outside and stopped to have a little talk with him. He was a handsome intelligent fellow with a very pleasing expression, and in a few minutes we were talking and laughing like old friends. "How far is it to Zennor?" I said; "I'm walking there." He answered that it was exactly five miles from his door. "Then," I returned, "I wish you could tell me how to get there without going through the intervening space." He looked strangely puzzled. "Well" he began, and then stopped and cast down his eyes. "Really—I don't quite see" he started again, and again stopped, more puzzled than ever. Then he made a desperate effort to grapple with the problem. "You see, it's this way," he said; "the space is there—you can't get over that, and so I can't quite make out how——" But I was sorry to see him distressed and changed the subject, to his great relief.

I was told by the vicar of a parish I was staying in that one had always to remember that the Cornish people take what is said literally; if you forget this and, inadvertently make use of some little figure of speech so common in conversation that it is hard not to use it, you are apt to get into trouble. The vicar himself, after twenty years' intimate relations with his parishioners, was liable to little slips of this kind, as I found. One day when I was there a man from a neighbouring hamlet came to the village and by chance met the vicar. "Why, Mr. So-and-so," exclaimed the latter, shaking hands with him, "it's a hundred years since I saw you!" Then after a little friendly talk they separated. But that unlucky phrase stuck in the man's mind, and he spent most of the day in going into the houses of all his intimates in the village and discussing the subject with them. "He said it were a hundred years since he saw me—now what did parson mean by that?" When, anxious to make a little mischief (having nothing else to do), I reported the matter to the vicar, he slapped his leg angrily and exclaimed, "That's how it is with them! There's an instance for you!" But it was a very delightful one, and in another moment his vexation vanished in a burst of laughter.

One might imagine that such misunderstandings simply result from stupidity. It is not so, unless we say that stupidity is nothing but the want of that sense which acts on our social intercourse much as the thyroid gland does on the bodily system, or, to take another image, like that subtle ingredient of a salad which "animates the whole." Curious to say, the most striking instance I met with of this want was from a man of that unpleasant class who must be forever doing or saying something to raise a laugh. They are found everywhere, even in Cornwall, and are common as is the "merry fellow" described over a century ago in the *Rambler*—the man whose ready hearty laugh and perpetual good humour and desire to say something to make you happy proceed from his high spirits. He is quite tolerable: the would-be witty or humorous person, the clown in the company, determined to live up to his reputation, is rather detestable, and reminds one of the actor who can never be himself, but is always posing to an audience even when alone with his wife, or nursing the baby when his wife is asleep.

I travelled with my Cornish funny man from Truro to Exeter, and as we talked the whole time I got to know him pretty well. He was a middle-aged, strong, good-looking fellow, and a good type of the shrewd, hard-headed Cornishman of the small-farmer class; he was a farmer and cattle-dealer, and had been head gamekeeper on a large landowner's estate. The trouble was that he prided himself on his wit and humour, or for what passes as wit among the people of his class, and, above all, on his good stories. He would now tell us a story, he would say, which would make us "die with laughing," and when it was received without a smile he was puzzled, and assured us that he had always considered it one of his best stories. However, he had others, plenty of them, which we would perhaps think better; but these were better only because they were coarser and more plentifully garnished with swear words, and in the end the other passengers—two or three grave elderly gentlemen, who had an armful of books and papers to occupy their minds—refused to listen any longer. He then gave it up, but being of a social disposition he continued to converse with me in a quiet sober way, but there was now a little cloud on his countenance, which had been so sunny before, as if our want of appreciation had hurt him in a tender part. The hurt had, perhaps, made him quarrelsome; at all events we presently fell out over a very trivial matter. We were discussing the scenery through which we were passing when he remarked on the prettiness of a scene that came before our eyes and I agreed; but by-and-by when he used the same expression about another scene I disagreed. "Do you not then see anything to admire in it?" he asked, and when I said that I admired it he wanted to know why I refused to allow that it was pretty after having called something else pretty because I admired it? He began to harp on this subject and to grow satirical, and wanted to know of every scene we passed whether I called it pretty or not, and if not why not. My replies did not seem to enlighten him much, and at last in a passion he begged me to tell him in plain language, if of two scenes we both admired one was pretty and the other not pretty, why he called them both pretty. I answered that it was because he had a limited vocabulary.

He threw himself back in his seat and looked at me as if I had struck or insulted him, then exclaimed, "Oh, that's it—I have a limited vocabulary!" and presently he added bitterly, "This is the first time in my life that I have been charged with having a limited vocabulary." Without saying more he got up, and going into the corridor planted his elbows on the sill and supporting his head with his hands, stared gloomily at the landscape for about a quarter of an hour. Then he came back to his seat and looked at me with a different countenance; the expression of sullen resentment had changed to a quite friendly one, but overcast with something like regret or shame, and speaking in a subdued manner he said, "You are right, and I deserved it. I know it is a great fault in me, but I assure you that when I use bad words in conversation I mean no more harm than—what shall I say?—than a woman when she says, 'Oh, bother it!' or 'Drat the thing!' because she can't fasten her blouse or her belt. 'Pon my soul I don't! It's just a way I've got into, and the words you didn't like slip out without my knowing it." And so on, with much more in the same apologetic strain. After that there was peace between us. I was indeed rather sorry to lose him at Exeter: as a "funny man," without a sense of humour, he had greatly entertained me, and wishing him well, I hoped he would continue in his mistake about a "limited vocabulary" in the sense in which he had taken the phrase.

My friend the vicar, who made the mistake of saying it was a hundred years since he had seen someone, told me one day that he had been attending a meeting of the clergy of the district, and finding himself in conversation with three friends who were all Cornishmen of good old local families, it occurred to him that it was a good opportunity to find out what educated men in the county would have to say on such a subject. The question, did the Cornish people have a sense of humour? took them by surprise; they had never considered it—it had never come before them until that moment. After some discussion it was decided in the affirmative; the Cornish *have* a sense of humour, but—a very important but—it is not the same as the sense of humour in the English people. English humour, they said, fell flat in Cornwall, even where it was seen, or guessed, that the words spoken were intended to be humorous. If they laughed or smiled, it was out of politeness or good nature, just to please you. And as our humour failed with them, so did theirs fail with us: we did not appreciate it simply because it was impossible for us, being Englishmen, to see it as they did with their Cornish minds.

A local writer, the late J. T. Tregellas, who wrote funny poems in dialect, and surveyed life generally from the comic point of view, has a considerable reputation in the county. In one of his works, entitled *Peeps into the Haunts and Homes of the Population of Cornwall* (Truro, 1879), his avowed intention is to "place before the reader a tolerably exact picture of a Cornishman as he is, with all his rough sense of honour, his kind heart, his self-reliance, his naiveté, his ingenuity, and his keen quiet power of wit and observation." There are scores of more or less funny stories in this book, but one is soon weary of reading it, because there is little or no evidence in it of the "keen quiet power of wit" one looks for. One finds what may be described as primitive humour—the humour of children and of men in a low state of culture who delight in practical jokes, rough banter, farcical adventures, grotesque blunders and misunderstandings and horse-play. Of unconscious humour there are many examples, which undoubtedly shows a sense of humour in the narrator: and I will quote the conclusion of one of the tales, perhaps the gem of the book, in which an old widow relates her three matrimonial ventures.

"And then I married a tailor who did praich sometimes, and was a soort of a teetotaler in his way, and never drinked nothing but tay and sich like; and then he faded away to a shaade, and this day three weeks he died; and ater he was dead they cut un oppen to see what was the matter with un. But waan of the young doctors that helped to do ut towled me that he died all feer and they couldn't find nuthin in un but grooshuns [sediment]. I woan't have nothin' of that soort agen, but I'll get a farmer with a little money; and so I oft to, for I've got twenty pounds a year and a house to live in."

Books of this kind do not help us much; they are, on the contrary, apt to be misleading when the author has an intimate knowledge of the people and dialect—and, besides, a little invention.

There are, I take it, two common sorts of unconscious humour; one into which persons who may be of humorous minds are apt to tumble through thinking too quickly and being too intent on their point, and who in their haste snatch at any expression that offers to illustrate their meaning without considering its suitability. The result may be a bull or a mixed metaphor. An Irishman, asked to define a bull, after a moment's thought replied, "Well, if you were to see two cows lying down in a field, and one was standing up, that could be a bull." A Cornishman would be incapable of such a reply; or of the Irishman's retort when his companion, accused of being drunk, protested that he was sober: "If ye was sober ye'd have the sinse to know ye was dhrunk." He makes no bulls and, does not know what they are. His unconscious humour is of the second kind, which consists in saying things in a way which would be impossible to any person possessing a sense of humour. Here is an example:

At St. Ives, one Sunday, I went to a Methodist chapel to hear a woman preach—a missioner or gospeller, I think she was called. I did not find her a Dinah, for she was rather large and stout, of a high colour, with black eyes and hair. But it was a singularly intelligent and sympathetic face, and to hear her was a pleasure and a relief, for it was on the eve of the last general election, when all the Little Bethels of Bolerium were being put to strange uses and pulpits were the rostrums of enraged politicians in white ties. She, sweet woman, preached only religion pure and simple in a nice voice without hysteria and with a charming persuasiveness. To hear her was to love her. A few days later she left the town, and then one who was interested in her work rushed in to the minister of the chapel to ask how many souls she had won for Christ on this occasion. For she had on previous visits been very successful in making converts. "Not one this time," answered the minister. "We were too busy with the elections."

A remark by one of the fishermen at a small coast village near Land's End about Brett, the marine painter, affords another pretty example of the native unconscious humour. Brett's outspoken atheism and brusque manners greatly offended the fisherfolk, and when he began work they watched him very narrowly, curious to know what kind of picture so extraordinary a person would produce. It astonished them to see him use his palette-knife instead of a brush to put on paint and spread it over the canvas. They had never seen such a method before, and it appeared to them wrong or not a legitimate way. One day on the beach they were discussing the strange artist within their gates with reference to some fresh cause of offence on his part, when the remark was made by one, "What can you expect of a man who says there's no God and paints his pictures with a knife?"

Here is another instance from Penzance. There is a public garden in the town, with beds of flowers, benches, a bandstand, a fountain, and at one side some tall elm trees with a rookery. The little fishes in the basin of water attracted a pair of kingfishers, and they haunted the gardens, flashing a wonderful blue in the eyes of the people. But they took the fry—the little sickly fishes which had cost the town several shillings—and the Town Council forthwith had them destroyed. I should have said that only in a Cornish town could so abominable an instance of philistinism be found had I not witnessed an even worse one when staying at Bath, when the Corporation of that noble town ordered the killing of the kingfishers that frequented the old Roman baths.

After the kingfishers had been destroyed at Penzance, the question of the rooks came up for discussion, and it was resolved to shoot the birds and pull the nests down; but here, as I was informed, the town clerk intervened and pleaded so eloquently for the birds that they were spared. Now one day a group of old men, habitués of the gardens, were sunning themselves there and discussing this question of the rooks. The birds were there, repairing their old nests in the elms with a good deal of caw, caw. They were as talkative as the old men, but "deep in their day's employ" at the same time. Joining in the conversation, I expressed my opinion of the councillors for wanting to destroy the rookery, and was asked indignantly by one of the old men how I would like it if, on a Sunday on my way to chapel in a black coat and silk hat, I were to pass under the rookery and something were to happen to my hat. I replied that I always attended chapel in tweeds and that if I wore a silk hat it would serve me right to have something happen to it. Such an occurrence would only afford an additional reason for preserving the birds. My questioner glared at me, and I judged from their looks that the others did not approve of such sentiments.

It was very funny, but I heard an even funnier one when listening to the talk of a knot of elderly and middle-aged men discussing the treatment the Education Bill was receiving in the House of Lords. But it was not in Penzance, and I will mercifully conceal the name of the little town in Bolerium where I heard it. The men, it must be observed, were all Methodists who had adopted the view of the question which the ministers had been expounding in the chapels. "What we want in England," said one, "is the Russian system, just to remove the men in the two Houses who are opposing the will of the people." The sentiment was heartily applauded by all the others. It was delightfully Cornish—just the sentiment one would expect to hear from the deeply religious Cornishman.

At this same place I heard about a local preacher, a man of a very fine character, who was taxed one day by his employer with having served as a model to an artist of the town, a Mr. Charles. "Yes," he said, "I have been sitting to Mr. Charles, and have had a good deal of conversation with him." Then after a long interval of silence he added, "Yes, I have been sitting to him. Mr. Charles has religion, but it is very, very, very, very, very deep down."

This appeared to be a clue worth following up, and I at once sought out this man and was delighted to know him; he was, physically and mentally, a type of all that is best in the Cornishman, but after a long talk on many subjects with him I was convinced that he was without the sense of humour. At the same time I felt that this was scarcely a defect in one of his nature. I felt, too, that something like this might be said of the people generally—the sense which they lack seems less important in their case than in that of others; it is not so much missed—because of their perennial vitality, their fresh impressible mind and sense of eternal youth and curious interest in little things which never fades and fails. Here I made the acquaintance of four men whose respective ages were eighty-one, eighty-five, eighty-six, and eighty-eight. There was no sign of weariness in any of them; they were as much alive and in love with life as their middle-aged neighbours and as the young, down even to the children.

These general reflections bring back to mind yet one more incident bearing on the point—an example of the buoyant child surviving in a man well advanced in years.

I had wasted a day indoors at Penzance reading books when, hearing the hour of four strike, I flew out for a walk to the neighbouring hills before dark. Hurrying along the street, which led me away from the front,

I felt that I wanted my afternoon cup of tea and thought I had better get it before quitting the town. I soon came to a small baker's shop, and going in and pushing open the door at the back discovered the baker and his family just sitting down to their tea. The women made room for me at the table and spoke welcoming words, while the baker himself looked at me but said nothing. He was a fine specimen of a Cornishman: old and strongly built, with a large perfectly bald head, on which he wore a skull-cap, and a vast cloud of white hair which covered the lower half of his face and flowed over his chest. He had the broad head, high cheek bones, large mouth and depressed nose, wide at the nostrils, of the pure Cornish Celt, and, most marked feature of all, the shrewd, prying, almost inquisitorial, yet friendly, blue-grey eyes. Those eyes, I observed out of the corners of mine, were furtively watching me, but I did not resent it. By-and-by I caught sight of another member of the family I had not observed before also watching me very attentively with the most brilliant eyes in the world—a fine grey parrot in a big tin cage at the far end of the room. He was standing at the open door of the cage, silent and motionless, with his neck craned out in a listening attitude. I went over to him and gave him some cake, which he accepted in a gentle manner and began eating. Then, coming back to my tea, I began praising the bird, saying that I knew a lot about parrots and admired and respected them because they were nearest to our noble selves in intelligence, and that I had never seen a finer grey parrot than this one. He was silent with me: that was the parrot's way; he was like a wise man, very still and very observant of a stranger in the house; he would watch and listen to know what the strange person was like before declaring himself.

The old man did not smile nor speak, but got up, went to the cage, and taking the bird on his hand returned to his seat. Then began a lively game between the two: the parrot climbed over and about the man, was snatched up and tossed as a mother tosses her babe, and finally deposited on the big bald head from which the skull-cap had been removed. The parrot rubbed his feathered head over the shining pate and wiped his beak on it. Then followed a fight with lightning-quick thrust and parry, a finger and a beak for weapons, after which the bird was snatched up and popped, back down, on the table. There he remained some time, perfectly still, his feet stuck up in the air, but not pretending to be dead, for the brilliant white eyes were wide open, keenly watching us all the time. Finally the bird twisted his head round, and using his beak as a lever turned over on his feet, and was invited to kiss and be friends. This the bird did, pushing his way with careful deliberation through the cloud of beard so as to plant his kisses on the lips.

During the performance I could not help remarking a singular resemblance between man and bird: the same love of fun appeared in their bright, watchful, penetrating eyes; one had as much pleasure in the game as the other; they were, man and parrot, very much on a level, very like little children, and like children they were without a sense of humour.

Or perhaps it would be more correct to say that children's humour is rudimentary. Undoubtedly there are individuals who possess it in a higher or more developed state, just as there are children who possess the sense of beauty, an ear for music, and other faculties of the adult, but such cases are exceptional.

It chanced that just before my meeting with the old man of the parrot I had been discussing the subject of this chapter with a gentleman of culture in the district, a member of an old and distinguished Cornish family, who has worked in his profession among the people and knows them intimately. He demurred to my idea that his countrymen (of the lower ranks be it understood) were without the sense of humour, and he instanced their "love of fun" as a proof of the contrary. Mere love of fun, however, always strongest in children and animals, is not the same thing as that finer, brighter, more intellectual sense we are discussing.

But how strong the simple primitive love of fun is in the Cornish people may be seen at Christmas time in St. Ives in their "Guize-dancing," when night after night a considerable portion of the inhabitants turn out in masks and any fantastic costume they can manufacture out of old garments and bright-coloured rags to parade the streets in groups and processions and to dance on the beach to some simple music till eleven o'clock or later. This goes on for a fortnight. Just think of it, men, women and children in their masks and gaudy get-up, parading the little narrow crooked muddy streets, for long hours in all weathers! And they are Methodists, good, sober people who crowd into their numerous chapels on Sundays to sing hymns and listen to their preachers! It is fun, pure and simple, and if you mix with them and witness their gaiety and listen to their bantering talk and happy laughter you will not discover the faintest flicker of humour in it all, and if you have witnessed the people of some French, Italian or Spanish town amusing themselves in this fashion, the Guize-dance will seem like a poor, rude imitation of the carnival got up by children.

THE POETIC SPIRIT

THE naturalist's mental habit of always trying to get at the reason and hidden significance of things is apt to become a worry when he begins to look closely at his fellow-creatures with the object of finding out what they really are or what the character of this particular human family or herd is compared with that of some other herd which he has studied and thinks he knows. Or perhaps it would be nearer the mark to say that his anxiety to classify everything is the source of his trouble, when with a Réaumur's skill his curious mind would distinguish men according to their racial and temperamental characters. It vexes his little busy brain, which loves neatness and symmetry, that men are so various, so complex, that they have so many hidden meanings and motives and instincts—so many invisible threads in the woven texture of their natures, which occasionally shine out, yellow and purple and scarlet among the threads of sober grey, yet when looked at closely, or examined with a magnifying-glass, become invisible again. Either he must give up the quest and the task in despair or else go doggedly on with a sort of stupid courage, trying not to think that he is blundering all the time. It is consoling in a difficulty of this kind to recall the case of an eminent ethnologist, who was exceedingly industrious and prolific, and was very great a short generation ago, about which time his learned contemporaries, vexed at his facile method of overcoming all difficulties, rose up against and overthrew him, smashing and pulverising his beautiful theories. After which, with a very engaging, proud humility, he boasted that he had been the fool to rush in where the angels (his opponents) had feared to tread, and that to attack and overthrow they had had to follow him into new and wider fields where they otherwise would never have ventured. We must all be fools in the same way, if we have a little of that courage which I have called stupid, each in his own small sphere, and we certainly do a useful thing if, in exposing our thick skulls to knocks (which don't matter), we succeed in giving courage to better men.

If I had not been a fool, or had not troubled myself with this serious question, it would have been much pleasanter for me in my rambles at this end of all the land, seeing that the inferior animals are so very much   simpler and more easy to read than men. Those donkeys, for example, which I meet on the moor, and their scarcely less intelligent friends the jackdaws, I know them a hundred times better than I can know any man—even my own self. And the house-dog too, who is supposed to be mentally more like his masters than any other beast—this dog who watches my comings and goings out of the corners of his eyes and who thinks himself wonderfully clever when, knowing that I don't want him, he steals secretly off an hour before I go out and meets me (by chance) among the furze bushes a mile from home—do I not know every thought in his curly black head, if his little mental trick of putting two and two together can be called thought? And the gulls on the cliff—do I not know just how they will comport themselves; how each bird will eye me suspiciously, sideways, with one brilliant eye at a time; how they will rise and float and dwell on the air, or sit on a rock with beaks to the wind—do I not know every word they will say in their herring-gull language?

It is true they will now and then do a thing which will come as a surprise. Here is an example—an incident I have just witnessed. All day the wind had been blowing half a gale from the sea when I went down to the rocks to get a good mouthful of air before it was dark. There were the gulls at the usual spot; and no sooner had I climbed into a sheltered nook among the rocks than they were all up floating overhead, swooping and rising, and pouring out their insistent loud angry anxious cries. For they were just beginning to nest on the ledges of the cliff beneath me and were troubled at my presence. In spite of the very cold wind and the growing obscurity, when the sun had gone down, I kept my place for upwards of an hour, and for the whole of the time they continued soaring and screaming above me: now with extended motionless wings seeming not to move yet mounting all the time, higher and higher, until they would be four or five hundred yards above me and would begin to look very small; then down and down again in the same imperceptible way, but sometimes descending with an angry rush until they were no more than thirty or forty yards high and one bird among them would make a violent swoop to intimidate

me, coming to within a couple of yards of my head with loud swish
of wings and sudden savage scream. I noticed that the swoops were all
made by one bird, that this same bird acted throughout as fugleman
and leader, that whenever the others began to drift away, further and
further apart, and their cries grew fainter and less persistent, he or she
reanimated them and brought them back with a fresh outburst of fury,
emitting louder screams and dashing down in a more violent manner.
The longer I watched them the more wonderful appeared the difference
in disposition between this one bird, this white flying image of wrath,
and the others.

Now at intervals of about three or four minutes my attention would
wander from the gull to see and listen to a rock pipit that had its home at
that spot and was also nesting in a chink quite close to the gullery. Every
day and all day long, in all weathers, the little singer could be seen and
heard at that exposed spot, soaring up at intervals to a height of a couple
of hundred yards; then slowly falling back to the rocks; head down, tail
spread and wings pressed to its sides with the quills standing out—a
shuttle-cock or miniature parachute in figure; and while descending he
emitted the series of airy tinkling sounds that make his melody. And now,
in spite of the lateness of the hour and increasing gloom on the sea and
clouded sky and of the cold wind, the little creature would not desist from
its flight and song. Its little big passion was as strong and inexhaustible
as that of the enraged gull. Then occurred the incident I set out to tell:
the gulls with their prolonged monotonous wailing cries were balanced
in the air at a height of ninety or a hundred yards, their trumpeter and
inspirer keeping in the centre of the scattered company directly above my
head. The pipit shot up from the pile of rocks in which I was lying, and
rising obliquely from the land side reached the highest point of its flight
well over the sea, and then just as it set its feathers to begin its descent
a furious gust of wind caught and whirled it landwards, still emitting its
tinkling sound, into the very midst of the company of hovering gulls. No
sooner was it among them than the angry, alert leading bird, half closing
its wings, swooped down on the little tinkler, and instantly a frantic chase
began, with lightning-quick doublings, now over the sea, now the land,
the gull with its open beak almost touching the terrified little fugitive.
"Save yourself, pipit!" I exclaimed, for another inch and the small spotted
singer would have been in the big hungry yellow beak and flight and
tinkling song ended for ever. And in another moment the tension was
ended, for the little thing had gained the rocks and was safe: but it sang
no more that evening.

Now, strange as all this may seem—that the pipit should live and breed just by or among the herring gulls, ready at all times to seize and devour any living creature that comes by chance in their way, and that it should go on ascending and descending, singing and singing, every day and all day long, just where the gulls are perpetually floating and flying hither and thither, always on the look-out for something to devour—it is but acting in accordance with its known character. The small bird is without fear of its big rapacious neighbours: it has its own quickness and adroitness to save it from all natural dangers of winds and waves and killing birds; it was only the rare chance of that gust of wind striking it just when it paused in mid-air before dropping, and carrying it away sideways into the midst of the herring gulls, which so nearly cost it its life. On the following morning the gulls would be there, flying about hungry as ever, and the pipit would go on with flight and song in the same old way, free as ever from apprehension. And as with the pipits so it is with all creatures that are preyed upon: sudden violent death as the result of any failure, or mistake, or slight accident, is a condition of wild life, else its vigour would not be so perfect and its faculties so bright.

Every day, in fact, when I am observing the actions of birds, or of animals generally, from a dog or a donkey to a fly, I may witness something unexpected, an action which will come as a surprise; but this will be only because of its rarity, or because it comes about through a rare concurrence of circumstances, but not because the creature has acted in any way contrary to its nature.

It is sadly different (sadly, I mean, for the naturalist) with regard to human beings. You cannot generalise from the actions of an individual as you may safely do in the case of a titlark or a gull or a donkey. You study a dozen or a hundred, and then begin to think that you have not had a sufficient number owing to the variety you have noticed, and you study a hundred more and after all you are still in doubt. It may appear that, in the last chapter, I have not shown much doubt as to the want of a sense of humour (as we understand it) in the Cornish. I have not; but when it comes to another and a greater faculty—imagination, to wit—I am not very sure.

If it could be taken for granted that a people who have never produced any artistic or literary work worth preserving are without imagination, to use the word in its higher sense, as the creative faculty, the question would be a very simple one, seeing that Cornwall has given us nothing or next to nothing. Compare it in that respect with the adjoining county, divided from it by a little river, but distinct racially: what lustre Devon has shed on the whole kingdom! how many of her sons are so great in arms and arts, above all in literature, that we regard them as among the immortals; and what a multitude of lesser men who have made us richer in many ways! Now as one with a very superficial knowledge on this subject I have put the following question to the three men of my acquaintance who have the widest knowledge of English poetic literature: "Has Cornwall ever produced a poet?" and in each case came the quick reply, "Yes, Hawker of Morwenstow." Now Hawker is a great man to us on account of his strong and original character, but he was a very small poet; I should say that during the last half-century England has always had twenty or thirty living minor poets who rank high above him. Finally, he was not a Cornish but a Devon man, and it therefore struck me as exceedingly curious that I should have had that same answer from the last of the three friends interrogated, seeing that he is himself a highly accomplished poet, a Devonian whose birth place is just on the borders of the duchy. The reply, "Yes, Hawker of Morwenstow," may then be taken to mean "No, not one."

Nevertheless, it cannot be said that Cornwall has contributed absolutely nothing to literature. I have already sung the praises of Richard Carew's work; but he was a prose writer—he failed pitifully when he attempted verse; he therefore stands on a lower level, with perhaps two or three more who have written good prose—William Scawen and Borlase, the antiquary, may be mentioned. But there is Thomas Carew, the lyrist, and friend of Donne, Suckling and Ben Jonson—if he may be called a Cornishman. His name is not included in Boase and Courtney's monumental *Bibliotheca Cornubiensis*, in the preface of which work they courageously say, "The writers of Cornwall bear no inconsiderable place in the literature of their country." But if we take it that this Carew was a Cornishman, though born out of the county, we must admit that Cornwall has produced one good poet. He does not count for very much, however—this one poet who lived three centuries ago and wrote half a dozen little things that sparkle like diamonds—seeing that he was of that class which is never native, of the soil. Even in those old days men of birth did not spend their lives at home; they attended the court and went forth wide in the world wonders for to see, and inter-married with families outside of their own class, so that, like the Jews among us, they were and always are, racially as well as socially, a distinct people among the people. Norman and Saxon and Dane are we, says the poet truly enough, and he might have added Celt, but the mixing process has been infinitely greater in the upper ranks. The Cornish people, I take it, are Celts with less alien blood in their veins than any other branch of their race in the British Islands.

One day in a village street I met a fine athletic looking oldish man with a very marked characteristic Cornish face, but painted by alien suns to deepest brown, and that colour of the tropics contrasted oddly with the bright blue-grey eyes and reddish-grey beard. He laughed when I said that I supposed he was a stranger there. Yes, a stranger in a sense, he said, since he had been away over forty years, working in the mines, in America, Africa and Australia. But his forty years' labour had not hurt him much; he felt young still and was going back to Queensland after a little look round. For one thing he had never touched alcohol in his life and he would like to pit his strength against that of any man of thirty in that village where he was born sixty-seven years ago. Yes, it was his own native place which he had come back after forty years to have a look at. His people were there still, and had been there to their certain knowledge over six hundred years. And I dare say, he added, if we knew all we could say a thousand.

Five or ten thousand would perhaps have been nearer the truth. And so it is with the common people generally. They have become great roamers nowadays; they go forth in hundreds every year into all parts of the world, but they appear to cherish the old Cornish feeling against marrying among strangers; they return after few or many years to find wives, and that, I conjectured, was the old miner's motive in coming back to his village "just to have a look round." One of the saddest things in this perpetual going and coming is that a great many men, young and in the prime of life, return after contracting miner's disease, usually in Africa; and though it is known to everyone that they are doomed men, they marry and live just long enough to leave a child or two before they are gathered to their fathers.

To return to the main point. Is this surprising dearth of the creative faculty, or of genius, in art and literature a good criterion—does it justify us in saying that the people are devoid of imagination?

For an answer one can only go to the people themselves not to those of good birth who are in a sense foreigners, or different racially as we have seen, but to the true natives who remain from generation to generation on the land. We are told so often and so insistently by persons who speak with authority that the Celts are an imaginative people that we come to regard it as an established fact, beyond controversy, as true, for instance, as that the blood of a dark-haired person is heavier than the blood of a blonde. It consequently came to me as a great surprise to find that a people so markedly Celtic as the Cornish were the most prosaic I had ever known. At first I could not quite believe that it was so: it was only that I was a stranger among them and had not yet found the way to the hidden romantic vein and poetic spirit in them. Gradually it was borne in on me that the vein was not there, that it had no existence—that my wish and no secret living spring or hidden treasure in the earth had caused the hazel twig to dance and dip in my hand. Or, if they had it, then, like their sense of humour, it was of that lower or undeveloped root kind discoverable in children and in primitive people.

Undoubtedly this is contrary to the conclusion any person would most probably form on a first and superficial acquaintance with the people, on account of their manner and disposition, in which they differ so greatly from the more stolid, slower-moving, thinking and speaking English peasant. Nevertheless in the English peasant in the north, south and Midlands, in spite of that seemingly mental and physical heaviness and absorption in the purely material things which concern him in his struggle for existence, I have found that hidden vein of romance and that poetic feeling which I have failed to find in West Cornwall.

On this subject I do not venture to speak of the Cornish people generally. There may be important differences. I have been told that in the more easterly parts, particularly in mining districts, the people are not of so lively, friendly and communicative a disposition as in West Cornwall; but I assume that here, in Bolerium, we get the least mixed, the truer, Cornishman. Here it seemed to rile that not only with regard to the æsthetic faculties, but in various other ways too, in mind and disposition, they are like children of a larger growth. On this point, however, one may very easily go wrong, since the same thought will sometimes strike us with regard to other Celtic families. Yet in Cornwall I could not get away from the idea that the child-like traits in the character of the people were not merely a matter of disposition, of the buoyant child surviving in the man, but that it marked a lower stage in mental development. This may be wrong: but after all what one wants is a working theory, and it does not very much matter whether it be true or false so long as it enables us to get over the ground.

When we live with savages, or uncivilised people, it is very much like living with children; we get to know them as we never know the civilised beings we spend our lives with although they are our own people. For however unexpected their changes of temper and actions may be, especially where these place us in sudden peril, we yet know that they are only feeling, thinking and acting in accordance with their true natures.

They are not quite so simple and easy to read as the lower animals; nevertheless the difference between the uncivilised and civilised man is so immense that we can say of the first that it is as easy to understand him as it is to understand a dog or a donkey or a child.

It may also be observed that there is a vast difference in this respect between the members of separate classes in the same community, in spite of their racial relationship—between peasant and gentleman; and it may perhaps be taken as a truth that complex conditions of life make complex characters. The Cornish peasant appeared to me easier to understand than the English, and, as I imagined, because he was nearer, mentally, to the child. It may even be that the greater sympathy with children of the Cornish people, men and women, is due to this fact that man and child are nearer in mind than is the case with the English people. They are moved emotionally in the same way as children and are liable to gusts of passion, and, like children, are apt to be cruel in their anger. They are candid, pliant and delighted to serve you when pleased; but are subject to petulant and stubborn fits, and will brood in sullen resentment for days, meditating revenge, for some trivial imaginary slight. And they are intensely fond of things which please children—gifts, shows, gay colours, noise and excitement. Here is a little characteristic incident in which we see the bad stubborn boy surviving in the adult. The late Royal Academician, Hook, was on the sands at Whitesand Bay working at a sea-piece when two natives came up and planted themselves just behind him. There was nothing the artist hated more than to be watched by strangers over his shoulders in this way, and pretty soon he wheeled round on them and angrily asked them how long they were going to stand there. His manner served to arouse their spirit and they replied brusquely that they were going to stay as long as they thought proper. He insisted on knowing just how long they were going to stay there to his annoyance, and by-and-by, after some more loud and angry discussion, one of them incautiously declared that he intended standing at that spot for an hour. "Do you mean that?" shouted Hook, pulling out his watch. Yes, they returned, they would not stir one inch from that spot for an hour. "Very well!" he said, and pulled up his easel, then marching off to a distance of thirty yards, set it up again and resumed his painting. And there within thirty yards of his back the two men stood for one hour and a quarter, for as they did not have a watch they were afraid of going away before the hour had expired. Then they marched off muttering curses.

In all this, and still more in their occasional emotional outbreaks, which when produced by religious excitement are so painful to witness, the Cornish are no doubt very much like other Celts in Britain; but in some things, with one of which alone I am concerned here—to wit, the imaginative faculty—these separate branches of the race have diverged very widely indeed. The old literatures of Ireland and Wales live to show it, and in Ireland, at all events, this fountain of inspiration has never ceased to flow. It is flowing copiously as ever now, and making us richer every day. What is the secret of this great difference—the reason of this creative faculty which has given Ireland, in spite of her misery, so splendid a place in our literature, which appears like a touch of rainbow colour in the humblest peasant's mind, and does not exist and never has been in Cornwall? Doubtless from that mixture of blood which came to pass in Ireland during those restless centuries of tremendous changes, when ancient nations were cast into another mould, of emigration and conquest and colonisation; and of the fusion of races by intermarriage, of the Irish Celts with the mentally more virile and imaginative invaders from the north. We must assume, too, that this fusion of blood did not go so far and hardly took place at all in Cornwall. We see that the conquerors left but few and slight traces of their occupancy in the peninsula, and the presumption is that they did not take root in it, that when they had come and conquered and had their carousal of blood they were glad to sail or march away, like William Gilpin in search of the picturesque, from a country of so barren and repellent an aspect, to seek for a permanent resting-place in a softer, more fertile land. Lord Courtney, in a presidential address to the Natural History and Antiquarian Society of Penzance, said:

> While the wave of conquest swept completely over other parts of England, it only just reached this part and then receded. The population of Cornwall in general has remained much more homogeneous, much more Celtic in type, than in other parts; and of all Cornwall there is no part like this in which we are met with probably so pure a breed of human beings.

The people were left in their rocky land, and what they had been—an ancient crystallised race with the imaginative faculty undeveloped—they remained and remain to this day.

It has been thought that because Cornwall is pre-eminently the land of strange beliefs and of old tales and legends relating to mythical saints and heroes, to giants and demons with a great variety of fantastic beings— mermaids, fairies, pigsies and piskies and other little people—the Cornish are a highly imaginative people. These things are old survivals, and are of the imagination in its childish or primitive stage. The belief in all these fanciful beings is pretty well dead and gone now; at all events, I was unable to find even an old woman who had anything to say of the old beliefs which was not disrespectful. But these beliefs undoubtedly kept their hold on the Cornish mind very much longer than in any other part of the country, and with these beliefs certain pagan, or Druidical, observances were also kept up, and have only died out within the last thirty or forty years. Similar beliefs and observances were as common all over England as in Cornwall; there was not a hill or down, or lake or stream, or singular tree or rock, which did not have its own special demon or genius. All this passed away with the fusion of the British Celts with a people in a more advanced psychological stage. But although these childish things have been put away so long, you will still find faint traces of them everywhere, even in the most Saxon districts in England. They inspire little or no belief, but are kept in memory, like old ballads, and passed on from generation to generation. In Cornwall belief in them continued to within very recent times, and they are remembered still. It was said not very long ago by a well-known Penzance writer that folklorists, when they come to Cornwall, especially the west, complain that the materials are so abundant they do not know how to manage them. Merely to enumerate and classify legends and beliefs in giants, little men, and fairies of a dozen denominations, ghosts, souls, semi-devils and phantoms of divers sorts, goblins, monsters and mermaids, is more than they can do. A very large number of these legends, enough, one would imagine, to satisfy the greatest enthusiast, have been collected by Robert Hunt in his *Popular Romances of the West of England*, and by William Botterell in *Stories and Folklore of West Cornwall*, in three series. There we have it, or as much of it as we want a huge crude mass, the rough material out of which an early literature might have come had there ever been a mind capable of assimilating and giving it literary form.

When the old language was in a moribund state during the seventeenth and early eighteenth centuries, there appeared to be but one man in the county to lament its passing—William Scawen, who loved the old things, old usages and traditions, and who rebuked his fellow-Cornishmen for their indifference with a bitter eloquence. But he did not grieve over the dying language on account of any noble or beautiful or otherwise valuable work enshrined in it. The few mystery or miracle plays and other native productions which existed (and exist still) were not worth preserving. What troubled him was the thought that the old ways and spirit were to a great extent dependent on the old tongue. The plays were valueless as literature and were of the same quality as a thousand more which were once performed in most parts of England, the loss of which nobody regrets, but their performance drew people together from all parts to the vast open-air theatre, the *plan-an-guare,* and in this way whatever little romance and poetry existed in the minds of the people was kept alive.

A mightier change was to come later, when Wesley made his descent on the county about the middle of the eighteenth century and converted the people wholesale to Methodism. This was in many ways the very worst form of religion for a people of the temper and character of the Cornish, but it suited them exactly at the time it came to them—a dull and stagnant period in their history when the Church was indifferent. They were a highly emotional race and were in a starved condition, hungry for some great excitement, some outlet for their repressed natures, some excuse for a mad outburst, and this gave it them—these wonderful gatherings of miners, fishermen and labourers on the land, in the old disused theatres under the wide open sky, listening to that mysterious supernatural man who had it in his power to call down God to them. That same God who had been growing further removed from their lives and dimmer in their minds for years and for generations, until He was little more than one of the Cornish giants or supernatural monsters believed in by the "old people"—now once more an awful stupendous reality, a gigantic kite hovering on broad black wings over their congregated thousands, his burning, rapacious eyes fixed on them, while from time to time he made his little tentative swoops to set them fluttering and screaming. For they were like terrified fowls and chickens in a farm yard, each expecting and dreading to be made a victim—each knowing that his miserable soul might not be saved until the winged terror fell upon him to grip and bury its crooked lacerating talons in his flesh. And when the stoop and grip came he rolled on the ground bellowing and shrieking to the accompaniment of groans and sobs and piercing cries of those around him. Dreadful as this was, and horrible and loathsome to witness by any person of a decent or reverent mind, it was yet a joy to them and gave them what they wanted—a glorious emotional feast. From the days of Wesley to the present time these unseemly spectacles have been common throughout the length and breadth of the peninsula, as they have been in Wales, and one may be thankful that the Irish kept the old faith, which does not permit such things, since it saved them from a like degradation.

I rejoice, and all who have any respect and love for humanity will rejoice, that in Cornwall at all events these exhibitions are declining.

Last year one day a Truro acquaintance of mine got into a railway carriage in which were five Methodist ministers returning from a conference they had been attending. They were discussing the decrease in the number of converts and the decline of revivals during the last few years. One of them, a stout, elderly person, said he did not take so pessimistic a view of the position as the others appeared to do. He thought the falling off, if there were any, was perhaps attributable to the ministers themselves, and then added, "All I have got to do is to preach my Judgment-Day sermon to set them howling." The others were silent for a little, and then one said, "Do you think it wise to say much about everlasting punishment at the present juncture?" No one replied to the question, and after an uncomfortable interval they changed the subject.

One would hardly suppose that the "present juncture" would be causing much anxiety in far Bolerium; yet even here in this ancient rocky fastness of Dissent the trumpets of the New Theology are beginning to sound in some of the chapels. Methodism, on account of its wealth and the perfection of its machine, will be the last of the sects to feel the impending changes; but this is a subject which does not concern us here, and enough has perhaps been said to show that Methodism with its revival campaigns and notion as to the necessity of sudden conversion, accompanied with the outward visible signs of the inner struggle and change—sobbings, howlings, contortions and Glory Hallelujahs—is not a healthy one for so extremely emotional a people.

Wesley's fame does not, however, suffer from these sad incidental results of his great propaganda. He remains a very great man, the greatest of all the sons of the Anglican Church, one who went about his work among Celts and Saxons indifferently in a white heat which set men's hearts on fire. He had no pleasure in seeing people carried so completely away by their feelings and behaving like lunatics or frenzied wild beasts in a cage; on the contrary, he abhorred the sight of such things even as he abhorred Dissent and that "odious familiarity with the Deity" which grieved and disgusted his reverent mind in his preachers. Nor did he consider, nor was it possible for him to know, in his long strenuous life, which was but a battle and a march, as the poet has said of another leader of men, while like the wind, homeless, without resting, he stormed across a world convulsed by a tremendous religious awakening and excitement—he did not know that he was inflicting a deadly injury on the Church which he loved above all things and clung to all his life long, and, finally, that in the end it would all make for ugliness.

This is indeed the chief cause of the repulsion with which Methodism and Nonconformity in general is regarded by those who have the sense of beauty, whose hearts echo the poet's cry:

> Beauty is truth, truth beauty: that is all
> Ye know on earth, and all ye need to know.

There is one God; but the gods which men worship are innumerable as the stars in heaven and as the sands on the seashore, and they vary in character even as their worshippers do. To go back to the dark days of the seventeenth century, we see that beauty and whatever was of good report, which became associated in the Puritan mind with the life and forms of worship of their enemies, was a thing accurst. And, the human mind being what it is, it was but natural that the particular god of their worship came to be the very god of ugliness, a despiser of beauty who looked with jealousy on those who were won by it even as he did on those who kissed their hands to the rising moon. He was not the God to whose glory the great fanes of England were raised. And from that far time of Oliver's usurpation when all monumental things became despicable this same temper of mind and dismal delusion has come down to us in a hundred denominations with their temples of ugliness sprinkled over all the land.

Any house is good enough to worship God in, is a treasured saying, and it has been remarked that no place of worship has ever been raised by Nonconformity in England which any person would turn aside from the road to look at. This would be too little to say of the chapels in West Cornwall, where the principle of any-house-good-enough has been carried to an extreme. The principle may or may not be insulting to a personal Deity, mindful of man and anxious that man should do Him honour—we cannot know *His* mind on such a question; but these square naked granite boxes set up in every hamlet and at roadsides, hideous to look at and a blot and disfigurement to the village and to God's earth, are assuredly an insult to every person endowed with a sense of beauty and fitness. You will notice that a cow-house or a barn or any other outbuilding at even the most squalid-looking little farm in a Cornish hamlet strikes one as actually beautiful by contrast with the neighbouring conventicle. And in a way it is so, being suited to its purpose and in its lines in harmony with the surrounding buildings, with the entire village grouped or scattered round the old church with its dignified old stone tower, and finally with the rocky land in which it is placed. From such a building—barn or cow-house—one turns to the chapel with a feeling of amazement, and asks for the thousandth time, how can men find it in them to do such things?

The interior of these chapels is on a par with their exterior appearance. A square naked room, its four dusty walls distempered a crude blue or red or yellow, with a loud-ticking wooden kitchen clock nailed high up on one of them to tell how the time goes. Of the service I can only say that after a good deal of experience of chapel services in many parts of England I have found nothing so unutterably repellent as the services here, often enough conducted by a "local preacher," an illiterate native who holds forth for an hour on the Lord's dealings with the Israelites in a loud metallic harsh Cornish voice.

I observed that as a rule but few adults attended the morning services in the villages and small towns; the women had their housework to do and dinner to cook; the men liked a long rest on a Sunday morning, and did not care to wear their best suit of clothes the whole day. These all flocked to the afternoon or evening services; but alas for the little ones!—they were all packed off to chapel in the morning. Again and again on taking my seat in a chapel at the early service I found myself in a congregation chiefly composed of children. What can be the effect on the child mind of such an interior and of such a service—the intolerable sermon, the rude singing, the prayers of the man who with "odious familiarity" button-holes the Deity and repeats his "And now, O Lord" at every second sentence—the whole squalid symbolism! One can but say that if any imagination, any sense of beauty, any feeling of wonder and reverence at the mystery of life and nature had survived in their young minds it must inevitably perish in such an atmosphere.

WINTER ASPECTS AND A BIRD VISITATION

HAVING finished, not very satisfactorily perhaps either to myself or readers, with the difficult subjects which occupy the last few chapters, I returned with renewed zest to my solitary rambles among the hills and along the coast, particularly to that most fascinating strip of country named "Cornwall's Connemara." It was going back to the land and the simple life in a fresh sense—to have moorland donkeys and conies, and daws, gulls and yellowhammers, instead of men for company; creatures whose lowly minds do not baffle us. I doubt if even the wildest American of "the new school of natural history" would maintain that these friends in fur and feathers possess the faculty of imagination in any degree. It was very pleasant and restful to sit on a granite boulder on the hillside and gaze by the hour, thinking of nothing, on the blue expanse of ocean and the more ethereal blue of the sky beyond, with perhaps a few floating white clouds and soaring white gulls in the void to add to the sense of height and vastness.

There is no question that the best days in the six months from October to March, which are more or less charged with gloom in these northern realms, are those rare days when the sky is clear, the wind still, and the sun floods the world with light and heat. Such days are apt to be warmer here than in other parts; even the adder, hibernating in his deep dark den beneath the rocks, is stirred by the heavenly influence, and crawls forth on a midwinter day to lie basking in the delicious beams. And the entire visible world, sea and land, is a glittering serpent, its discontent now forgotten, slumbering peacefully, albeit with wide-open eyes, in the face of the sun.

Here, in such weather, the futility of all our efforts, whether with pen or pencil, to convey the picture to another has forced itself on me. Some of the details in a description are visualised and remain, but refuse to arrange themselves in their proper place and order, and the result is a mere confusion. I can but go down to a distance of a mile or two from the hills and, turning my back to the sea, look at the prospect before me, and omitting all the small details speak only of its shape and colour. On the right hand and on the left it stretches away to the horizon, and it rises before me up to the rock-crowned peaks and ridges of the hills, the slopes and the moor below splashed and variegated with dead heath-brown, darkest green, and dull red, the hues of heather, furze and dead bracken; and everywhere among the harsh, rough, almost verdureless vegetation appear the granite boulders and masses of rock cropping out of the earth. A scene that enchants with its wildness and desolation; also, on wet days and when the air is charged with moisture, with its novel and strikingly beautiful colour.

The colour of bracken, living or dead—of a plant so universal and abundant—is familiar to every body, yet I would like now to dwell at some length on its winter colour because it is a strange thing in itself—one of the most beautiful hues in nature which appears in a dead and faded vegetation after the beech-like brilliant autumn tints of russet, gold and copper-red have vanished, and glows and lives again as it were, and fades and vanishes only to return again and yet again, right on to the time when the deep undying roots shall thrust up new stems to uncurl at their tips, spreading out green fresh fronds to cover and conceal that mystery, even as we cover our dead, beautiful in death, with earth and with green and flowering plant. This phenomenon is common enough, but in no place known to me is the landscape so deeply and so constantly coloured by dead bracken as on these slopes, on account of the great abundance of the plant and the excessive moisture in the atmosphere.

In other parts of the county where trees grow, a curious effect of the excessive humidity is seen in some woods, especially in deep valleys and coombes sheltered from the winds, in which the mists remain longest. Here you will find the trees thickly clothed from the roots to the highest terminal twigs with long coarse grey lichen like that which grows so abundantly on the granite boulders on the slopes and the rocks on the headlands. The trees are leafless but not naked in winter and look as if covered with a grey foliage, or grey with a faint tinge of green. The effect is not only singular; in walking through such a wood under the grey canopy of branches, and when you come out into an open glade and see the trees in multitudes extending far beyond and all clothed in the same dim mysterious unearthly colour, you are apt to have the fancy that you are in a ghostly wood and are, perhaps, a ghost yourself. Another singular and magnificent effect of dead bracken where it flourishes greatly among furze bushes can be best seen among the hills.

The first time I particularly noticed this effect was in April near Boldre, in the New Forest, a good many years ago. There was a patch of furze about three acres in extent, where the big rounded bushes grew so close as to touch one another and appeared to occupy the ground to the exclusion of all other plant life; yet it could be seen that bracken had also flourished there during the previous summer, growing tall among the bushes; for now the old dead and withered fronds were everywhere visible lying against or mixed with the dark massy spiky branch lets of the furze. Only it was so shrivelled and pale in colour, or rather colourless, amid the mound-like masses of the dark living green as almost to escape the sight. The mind at all events took no account of those thin and bleached lace-like rags of dead vegetable matter.

One day I walked in this place when it was raining, and after rain had been steadily falling for several hours; but the grey sky was now full of light and the wet grass and foliage had a silvery brightness that was full of promise of fair weather. The rain-soaked dead bracken had now opened and spread out its shrivelled and curled-up fronds, and changed its colour from ashen grey and the pallid neutral tints of old dead grass to a beautiful, deep rich mineral red. It astonished me to think that I had never observed the effect before—this marvellous transformation of the sere and almost invisible lace rags to these rich red fabrics of curious design spread upon the monotonous dark green bushes like deepest red cornelian or reddest, serpentine on malachite.

This peculiar beauty and richness of hue is seen in its perfection only while the rain is falling and the streaming water is glistening on the surface of the leaf, but is best when the rain is nearly over and the clouds are full of light. No sooner does the rain cease than the rich glistening red begins to grow dull and fades as the wet dries. In a little while, in a drying sun and wind, the red hue quite vanishes and the fern is again the old faded rag it was before.

In this part of West Cornwall there was more furze and bracken together than I had ever seen, where both plants grow in the greatest luxuriance, unmixed with other tree and bush vegetation, and with nothing among it but the grey lichened rocks which served to intensify the effect of the intermingled sombre green and glistening rich red. Nor had I long to wait for the falling drops which brought the loveliness into existence, seeing that it rains on most days, and when it was mild and the wind not too strong the rainy day was nearly as good as the rare golden day of clear skies and genial sunshine.

On one occasion when I was out in the hills feasting my sight on the beautiful strange aspect of things, when the rain was so heavy and continuous that it soaked through my waterproof and wetted me, I was surprised to find a lady artist at work under a big umbrella. She was one of a colony of forty or fifty artists in the small town close by, but the first one I had seen out in that wild place in wet weather. Her subject was a small, rather squalid-looking farm-house on the further side of a narrow green field—one which could have been better painted on a fine day. I was told that the artists of this one colony alone turn out about a thousand landscapes a year, and I wondered if anyone had ever attempted to paint that wonderful sight just at their threshold—the dead bracken among the furze with the silvery-grey rain on it.

On the higher slopes where the furze is less abundant the bracken predominates, covering large areas with its red tapestry, and on most days throughout the winter it keeps its deep strong colour, owing to the excessive amount of moisture in the air. It disappears only when the new fern springs and spreads a wave of monotonous green over the rough land and well-nigh obliterates all other plant life. Only at very long intervals there is another winter aspect of the hills and moors, when they are whitened with a heavy fall of snow. "About every ten years," people say; but although the weather was exceptionally cold in December 1906, I had no hope of witnessing that change, and going away to spend my Christmas elsewhere missed the very thing I wanted to see. It was not so much the sight of the hills in their ghostly white I desired as the accompanying phenomenon of the vast multitude of birds flying from the fury of winter; for whenever a wave of cold, with snow, comes over the southern half of England, the birds, wintering in myriads all over that part of the country, are driven further west, and finally concentrate on the Cornish peninsula and stream down to the very end of the land.

No sooner had I gone away than the bitterly cold weather with snow and sleet, which prevailed over a great part of the country at Christmas, swept over the southern and western counties and drove the birds before it. The first news I had of it was in a latter, dated December 30, from a naturalist friend, Mr. G. A. B. Dewar, who was, staying on the towans, overlooking St. Ives Bay, close to Hayle.

I wonder [he wrote] did you see much of the marvellous migration scene which took place here on Friday morning? For hours—till about midday—redwings, thrushes, larks and field-fares streamed across St. Ives Bay, coming from the east. There was a great highway of birds, which must have been miles broad. We saw them first from the window as we dressed. … Most of the birds crossed the Bay, going towards Land's End, but thousands and tens of thousands dropped exhausted among the sand dunes, or towans, here, and among these I found golden plover, ring plover, sanderlings, lapwings, etc.—altogether an extraordinary assemblage. On Saturday morning, lasting till one o'clock P.M., the birds returned in a great highway east again. Mingled among them were many small birds, linnets, etc. A most wonderful pathetic scene, I assure you. I wondered if any the travellers crossed the Channel, or whether they all stopped in this extreme westerly bit of land. I did not think England had so many fieldfares and redwings.

On my return a few days later, I found on inquiring along the coast that large numbers of the birds had appeared at the Land's End towards evening and settled down to roost in the furze and heath and among the stones. At one house, I was told, numbers of thrushes and starlings crowded on the window sills, and some of them that were stiff with cold were taken in, but were found dead in the morning. From all I could hear the migration appears to have spent itself at this spot.

To me the "pathetic" part of it was the reception the starved fugitives met with from the good people along the coast, especially at St. Ives with its horn or "island" beyond the town thrust out into the sea, a convenient, resting-place for the birds after flying across the bay. My information on the subject, which would fill some twenty pages of a Blue Book, was gathered from men and lads, mostly fishermen, who had taken part in the massacre. Each person buys a handful of small fish-hooks, manufactured for the purpose and sold, a dozen for a penny, by a tradesman in the town. Ten to twenty baited hooks are fastened with short threads to a string, two or three feet long, called a "teagle," and placed on a strip of ground from which the snow has been cleared. To these strips of mould or turf the birds fly and seize the hooks, and so blind to danger are they made by hunger that they are not deterred by the frantic struggles of those already hooked. Many birds succeed in freeing themselves by breaking the thread in their struggles, but always with that bit of barbed bent wire in their mouths or stomachs, which must eventually cause their death. In one garden where food was placed for the birds and their hunters kept out, eleven dead and dying birds were picked up in one day among the shrubs, all with hooks in their gullets.

One young fisherman told me with great glee that he had found two hooks besides his own in the mouth of a blackbird he had taken from his teagle.

This method of slaying the small birds, most common in seasons of snow and frost, and practised without a qualm by the pious natives of all ages, from the small shiny-faced boy to the hoary-headed ancient who can no longer take his seat in a boat—a method one would imagine which even the most hardened Italian, hungering for the flesh of robins, tom-tits and jenny-wrens, would be ashamed to follow—is not the only cruel and brutish one practised. Bush-beating is also common in many of the villages and hamlets along the coast and in the country generally. Even here at this extreme end of Cornwall, a treeless district, there are bits of hedge and sheltered spots with a dense bush growth to which birds resort in crowds to roost, and these are the places where bush-beating, or "bush-picking" as it is often called, is practised. It is a favourite pastime, men and boys going out in gangs with dark lanterns and sticks to massacre the birds. It is a primitive sort of battue with brooms and caps and jackets for weapons, and very many of the victims are lost in the dense thicket or in the surrounding blackness—little bruised and broken-winged birds left to perish slowly of cold and hunger and of their hurts.

Even more hateful than these battues and wholesale slaughter of the starving immigrants in times of severe weather is the little daily dribbling warfare which the boys are permitted to wage at all seasons in many villages and hamlets against the birds. They are actually encouraged to do it; and it is a common thing to find fathers and mothers, after a visit to their market town, giving little hooks and wire and steel gins to their small boys. Dolls for the girls and steel gins for the boys! Where there is a little strip of sand on the beach the gin is set, covered with a little sand, and a few crumbs strewn on it. One result of this practice is that many little birds after having been caught get away with the loss of a leg or foot. Every day at St. Ives I used to see one or more of these poor maimed creatures—sparrows, wagtails, rock and meadow pipits, and other species—painfully hopping on one foot or crawling with the help of their wings over the ground in search of food. Yet the boys and men who do these things every day and are not rebuked by their pastors and masters are, or are supposed to be, the spiritual children and descendants of John Wesley, who converted and made them what they are, the most religious people in Britain! Wesley, the most compassionate of men, who not only loved all creatures but actually believed that they too, like men, were destined to know a future life!

"One most excellent end may undoubtedly be answered by the present considerations," he said in concluding a sermon on this subject. "They may encourage us to imitate Him whose mercy is over all His works. They may soften our hearts towards the meaner creatures, knowing that the Lord careth for all."

I think if he could revisit the scene of his greatest triumph of over a century and a half ago; if he could stand, perched like a cormorant, on the rocky headland above the town on a misty Sunday morning in November or December, and look down on the numerous chapels and the people in their best black clothes thronging into them; if he could listen to their eager conversation as they went and know that they were greatly concerned about the precise differences between Methodist and Primitive Methodist, between Wesleyans, Bible Christians and the New Connexion, with other minute variations in form and shades of colouring; and if he then, casting his eyes down to where at the foot of the rock a faint, sharp, sorrowful little note is heard at frequent intervals, should catch sight of a maimed rock pipit or titlark, creeping painfully about the beach with the aid of its wings in search of small morsels of food among the shingle and sea-wrack, his soul would be filled with exceeding bitterness, "They do not know, they never knew me!" I think he would turn away from a people who call themselves by his name but are not his followers in that which was best in his teaching—not in that divine spirit of love and tenderness which was in Jesus of Nazareth, in St. Francis of Assisi, and in all men whose memories are sacred in the earth. I think he would pass away in the sea mist with a mournful cry which would perhaps be audible to the chapel-goers; and they would wonder at it and ask each other what this strange fowl could be that uttered a cry as of a soul in pain.

It is something to be able to say that not all of the inhabitants are indifferent to these things. Even in St. Ives, where bird-killing is most popular and a wholesale slaughter of the spent and hungry fugitives intoxicates with joy like a big catch of pilchards—where, indeed, bird-killing appears like an instinct as well as a pastime, having come down "from ancientie," to quote a phrase of Carew—there are some who are revolted by it. I am speaking not of visitors and English residents, but of native Cornishmen; and a few of these have begged me "to do or say something to put a stop to these disgusting barbarities"; and again they have said to me, "We can do nothing—they abuse us because we forbid them putting their traps and hooks on our ground—but you can perhaps do something."

Of these compassionate persons, of different social ranks, I will speak particularly of only one, a very tender-hearted woman, the wife of a working man, a huge fellow with the strength of an ox; and whenever the winter-driven birds arrived and were slaughtered in great numbers with circumstance of shocking cruelty, it was a consolation to her in her distress to think that he, her life-mate, although a native of the town, had never killed a bird in his life. There was doubtless a strain of mercy in both of them. She told me of an uncle who had inherited a house and garden in the town, where he had spent his life, whose habit it was to take out a basket of food every day for the birds. For some two or three years before his death one of his little pensioners was a robin with a crushed or broken leg that lived in his garden, and the woman assured me that when he was taken to be buried this bird followed the funeral, and was seen by many of those present flitting about close to the grave. On inquiry I found that this story was believed by many persons in St. Ives.

I have spoken in this chapter of the little crippled birds so often seen in this town and in some of the villages, and my belief was that these had all been caught in gins and had got away, leaving a foot or leg behind. But I occasionally saw a bird with a dangling leg, and could only account for it by supposing that in such cases the leg had been broken by a stone, the boys of the place all being greatly addicted to stone-throwing at the birds. Later I discovered that they were birds which had been caught in gins and liberated by their captors. At least a dozen of the big boys who spend all their leisure time in taking birds with gins on the sands at St. Ives assured me that they did not kill the small birds they caught, which were not wanted to eat. They killed starlings, blackbirds, thrushes and some other kinds, but liberated the wagtails, tit larks, robins and a few other small species. I also found out that when birds arrive in vast numbers in a severe frost or snowstorm and are caught with small baited hooks, many of the smaller birds after the hook has been taken from the mouth or gullet are allowed to fly away. One man, the most enthusiastic bird-catcher with the teagle in the place, after removing the hook from the mouth or gullet of the bird he does not want, takes the two little mandibles between his thumbs and forefingers and wrenches the face open, then tosses the bird up to fly away to a little distance, soon to drop down and perish in agony. Small birds that are not wanted, he says, will sometimes return after being liberated and get caught again; those he liberates will trouble him no more.

These things are perfectly well known to every one in the place, and as this man has not been taken by his fellow-townsmen to the cliff and stoned and his carcass thrown into the sea as food for dogfishes, but, on the contrary, as they have friendly relations with him and sit in the same chapel on Sundays and regard him as a respectable member of the community, one can only suppose that nothing in the way of cruelty to God's creatures can be hellish enough to touch the St. Ives mind.

But, as we know, there are some exceptions, and I must now go back to the compassionate woman and to a word she dropped when she spoke to me with tears in her eyes of these cruelties. "I'm sure," she said, "that if someone living here, who loves the birds, would go about among the people and talk to the men and boys and not be afraid of anything, but try to get the police and magistrates to help him, he could get these things stopped in time, just as Mr. Ebblethwaite did about the gulls."

But who was Mr. Ebblethwaite, and what was it he did about the gulls? I had been off and on a long time in the place and had talked about the birds with scores of persons without ever hearing this name mentioned. And as to the gulls, they were well enough protected by the sentiment of the fisherfolk. But it was not always so. On inquiry I found twenty persons to tell me all about Mr. Ebblethwaite, who had been very well known to everybody in the town, but as he had been dead some years nobody had remembered to tell me about him. It now came out that the very strict protection awarded to the gulls at St. Ives dates back only about fifteen to eighteen years. The fishermen always had a friendly feeling for the birds, as is the case in all the fishing places on the coast, but they did not protect them from persecution, although the chief persecutors were their own children. People, natives and visitors, amused themselves by shooting the gulls along the cliff and in the harbour. Harrying the gulls was the most popular amusement of the boys; they were throwing stones at them all day long and caught them with baited hooks and set gins baited with fish on the sands and no person forbade them. Then Mr. Ebblethwaite appeared on the scene. He came from a town in the north of England, in broken health, and here he stayed a number of years, living alone in a small house down by the waterside. He was very fond of the gulls and fed them every day, but his example had no effect on others, nor did his words when he went about day after day on the beach trying to persuade people to desist from these senseless brutalities. Finally he succeeded in getting a certain number of boys summoned for cruelty before the magistrates, and though no convictions followed nor could be obtained, since there was no law or by-law to help him in such a case, he yet in this indirect way accomplished his object. He made himself unpopular, and was jeered and looked black at and denounced as an interfering person, especially by the women, but some of the fishermen now began to pluck up spirit and second his efforts, and in a little while it came to be understood that, law or no law, the gulls must not be persecuted.

That is what Mr. Ebblethwaite did. For me it was to "say something," and I have now said it. Doing and saying comes to pretty much the same thing; at all events I have on this occasion kept Ruskin's words in mind concerning the futility of prodding and scratching at that thick insensible crust which lies above the impressible part in men unless we come through with a deep thrust somewhere.

The majority may hate me for having followed this counsel, but there will be one or two here and there who will applaud my courage for having spoken in this book of the ugly things as well as of the things which flatter. And I will add—in no boastful spirit, Heaven knows—that what I have written will not be forgotten to-morrow, nor next year, nor the year after, but will be read some day, with a sense of shame, I trust, by the children of the very men who could do something and that now, but who refuse to listen to me and others, or listen coldly, when we plead for the birds. I refer to the landlords, who are absent or else shut up and inaccessible in their houses where they see nothing and hear nothing; the local editors; the ministers of religion (God save the mark!); and, above all, the authorities, and county and borough councillors and magistrates. They are all very careful of their "position" and their "reputation" and cannot afford to and dare not denounce or interfere with these old pastimes or customs of the people, to which they are attached and upon which they look as a right.

A GREAT FROST

THERE was no second westward movement of birds in the winter of 1906–7 although another and more intense spell of cold weather occurred a month after the one described in the last chapter. It looked as if the birds had exhausted their powers in their long disastrous flight to and from the Land's End, or that some saving instinct had failed to come to them on this occasion. Doubtless many thousands had perished in that journey over a snow-covered country to the extremity of Cornwall, and we may suppose that when the weather moderated the surviving millions redistributed themselves over the southern counties from Somerset to Kent; also that many birds had been continually slipping away across the Channel. Many of our migrants, which have not a strict migration like the swallow and cuckoo, the species which shift their quarters or of which considerable numbers remain in this country throughout the year, do annually come down in batches to the south and remain for a month or so, in some cases until December, then vanish, and these no doubt continue their journey over the sea. Thus, every autumn there is a migration of goldfinches into Cornwall, many birds appearing in the neighbourhood of Mount's Bay in September and remaining until November. These goldfinches have a brighter plumage than those which winter in England, and appear to form a body or race distinct from the earlier migrants, having their own seasons and perhaps a route of their own.

To return to the great visitation of birds in December. I am sure that very many of these, exhausted by hunger and cold, dropped out of the winged army at the extremity of Cornwall, and remained there until the end of the cold season. At all events, when I returned to the scene in January, I noticed a very great increase in the number of wintering birds, particularly starlings, larks, song-thrushes, fieldfares and redwings.

The weather continued cold and rough, with storms of wind and sleet and occasional flurries of snow, until January 21, when the cold became intense, and that rare phenomenon in West Cornwall, a severe frost, began, which lasted several days, and was said by some of the old natives to be the greatest frost in forty years, while others affirmed they had not experienced anything like it in their lives.

I was staying at Zennor at the time—that lonely little village nestling among its furze thickets and stone hedges, with the rough granite hills, clothed in brown, dead bracken, before it and the black granite cliffs and sea behind. I had been amusing myself by feeding a few birds that came to the door, and now my small company of pensioners, suddenly grown tame, began to interest me very much. There was no garden to the house, which was situated in the centre of the village, with the church on one side and the inn on the other—nothing but the road, broadening out into a wide bare space on which my window, looked, with a stone hedge and a fountain of gushing water on the other side, where the people dipped their buckets and the animals came to drink. Here the cows came on their way to and from the farm, and the pigs and dogs and a flock of geese; and as some of these animals were always about, they very naturally helped themselves to the bread they found in the public road. Fortunately the ground-floor window had a raised stone platform before it, surrounded by iron railings, and I started putting out the food for the birds in this area. The cows and pigs could not get in there, but some of the most intelligent of the village dogs managed to get a share by thrusting their paws far in and dragging the scraps out, and the geese would follow suit, putting their long necks between the rails. The birds, however, fared better than before; thrushes, blackbirds, robins, dunnocks, pied wagtails, meadow pipits and one grey wagtail were the usual feeders; the daws, too, would occasionally pluck up courage enough to drop down between the railings and snatch up something.

One of my guests was a robin of exceptionally small size with a withered leg. This bird was first brought to me one evening by some of the children, who had caught it in the schoolroom, and thought I would be able to do something for it. A more pitiable object could not be imagined; it was nothing but a little feathered skeleton; the "comfortable little red waistcoat with legs to it" was now a sharp keel, but behind the bone one could feel the little muscular heart working away violently. One leg was crushed above the knee and was now dead and dried, the closed claws hardened into a ball. I assured them that nothing could be done to save it, that the most merciful thing we could do would be to let it fly away into the bushes, where it would quickly fall asleep and die without pain in the intense cold. I opened my hand and it darted away into the black bitter night, but great was my surprise next morning, when looking at the company gathered at the window, to find the wasted little cripple among them, eagerly picking up crumbs! I was foolishly pleased to see it there; nevertheless it was a pity that it had survived the night and in the end lived through the frost, seeing that a hopelessly injured and maimed bird is, like the caged bird, incapable of its proper life, and to anyone who can feel for a bird is better dead.

The second day of the frost made a wonderful difference in the appearance of the birds out in the fields, especially the starlings. These had now lost all energy and were seen everywhere moving languidly about over the pale frosty turf in a hopeless search for a soft place, while others were found gathered at some spot sheltered by a stone hedge from the bitter north-east wind, standing crowded together in listless attitudes, with drooping wings. By degrees the fieldfares and redwings disappeared. The song thrushes which, next to the starlings, were the most numerous, appeared to fare better than the other soft-billed species, owing to the abundance of snails in the stone hedges. It was a mystery to me how with nothing but those poor beaks they were able to get them out. Snails were exceedingly plentiful in the crevices between the stones, many of them easily got at, but so tightly were they glued and frozen to the stone that I could not pull them off with my fingers. They were like limpets on a rock, yet it was plain to see that the thrushes did get a good many out and so saved themselves from starvation. Their anvils were everywhere near the walls, each with its litter of broken shells about it. The hibernating snails were not only found in the stone hedges; they were also extraordinarily abundant among the sandhills or towans at Lelant and Phillack on the coast near St. Ives. They were hidden in the sand at the roots of the coarse marram grass growing on the hills. Here the thrushes had less difficulty in getting them out, and every stone lying in the sand was made use of. It amused me to find that the favourite anvil at one spot was a soda-water bottle which had been stuck deep in the soft sand, leaving the round end about two inches above the ground. Its form and the faint bluish tinge in the clear thick glass gave it the exact appearance of a round lump of ice, but the thrushes had discovered that it was not ice but something as hard as stone, and being immovable, better suited to their purpose than the pebbles and small fragments of stone lying about on the sand. All round the useful bottle the ground was thickly strewn with many-coloured broken snail-shells.

The soda-water bottle reminds me of the appearance of a singular and beautiful form of icicle which became common on the water-courses on the second and third days of the frost. I saw it chiefly on a stream near Zennor that gushes and tumbles over the rocks on its way to the sea and is in great part almost covered with a dense growth of dwarf blackthorn, bramble and furze bushes. Where the water pouring over the boulders splashes the overhanging branches, the constant drops running down the pendent twigs grew into globular or oval crystals; these were mostly about the size as well as shape of ducks' eggs, pure as the purest glass, and had the appearance of a wonderful crystal fruit hanging from stems on the dark purple-red sloe bushes.

I greatly liked to follow this same stream in its swift downward course, as it ran through the roughest bit of ground in all this roughest spot in West Cornwall, and where it finished its course, rushing down through a cleft into the sea, the sloping shore was abundantly strewn with masses of granite lying everywhere among the furze thicket, a spot where adders and lizards (the longcripple, as called here) are common in summer and a favourite refuge and dwelling-place of the fox. A fox belonging to this spot distinguished himself at one of the small neighbouring farms at the beginning of the cold spell. There were two small farm-houses very little bigger than cottages together, with nothing but a cart-road to divide them, and each one had its hen-house close by. The fox came, and the door not being properly fastened got in and succeeded in carrying away eight fowls besides injuring several more, without disturbing either the inmates of the house or the dogs. A few nights later he came again, and finding the door locked, turned his attention to the second hen-house. It was built of stone and the door was securely fastened, but it had a thatched roof, and getting on it he gnawed a hole big enough to let himself in. The fowls screamed, the dogs barked, and the farmer, roused from slumber, jumped out of bed and seizing his gun rushed out. Just as he got up to the hen-house he saw the fox pop up out of the hole in the thatch, leap down and vanish into the black night. Twelve fowls were found dead or dying of their bites as the result of this attempt, which was not a complete success.

The poor man was very much cast down at his loss when I saw him next day. "I've been feeding them all the winter," he said, "and they never laid an egg until now, and now just when they begin to lay the fox comes and kills them! If I go to the gentleman of the hunt he perhaps gives me a shilling a head at the outside, and perhaps nothing at all. He'll say, we're very sorry for you, but we can't do anything for you because the money isn't enough and you should take better care of your fowls." He went on in this mournful strain for about half an hour and said that what made it seem worse to him was the fact that the foxes had bred during the summer in the rocks quite near the farm, down by the sea, and he never disturbed them—never had a thought against them! I agreed that it was very hard lines and all the rest, but secretly my sympathies were with the fox rather than with him and his fowls.

It was certainly an almost incredibly audacious act on the part of the fox, seeing that in letting himself down through the hole he had made—"hardly big enough for a cat," the farmer said—he had put himself in a trap; yet in spite of the joyful excitement of killing and of the screaming and the fluttering of the birds, he became aware of the danger he was in and made good his escape. His mouth must have watered for many a day at the recollection of the fowls he had killed and left behind, and in the following month he actually came again one dark night and made a hole as before in the roof, and then smelling danger made off.

The day after the second raid I was down among the rocks and bushes by the sea, half a mile from the farm, when I heard the repeated angry croak of a raven not far away. He was perched on a rock on the further side of a gully a couple of hundred yards from me, and getting my binocular on to him I was surprised at his excited appearance, as I could see nothing to account for such a state. Presently he rose up to a height of about a hundred yards in the air, then turning and letting himself go he came down like a raven gone mad, violently doubling about this way and that in his descent until, nearing the ground, he struck savagely at a fox which I now perceived for the first time. A big gaunt-looking dog-fox standing motionless on a large rock rising about three feet above the surface. Just as the raven made the last sudden twist in his flight and delivered his blow the fox dropped flat down on the stone as if he had dropped dead, then, as the raven rose, he got up and stood again, motionless as before. Again and again the raven repeated the mad swoop, eight or nine swoops following in quick succession, and on every occasion the fox threw himself down just as the blow was struck, but invariably keeping his face towards the assailant with his mouth wide open and all his dangerous teeth displayed. Then the raven gave it up; he could not drive the fox from the big flat-topped rock on which he had placed himself apparently to defy the bird, and he knew, I imagined, that he was playing an exceedingly dangerous game. The extraordinary manner in which he twisted about in descending was evidently meant to intimidate and confuse his enemy and enable him to deliver his blow in an unexpected place, but there was danger in this method, seeing that the least miscalculation or the slightest accident would have placed him at the mercy of the savage beast hungry to get his sharp teeth into his hated black carcass.

The bird rose high up with a sullen croak and flew away out of sight, and only then the fox quitted his post. He did not see me among the rocks on my side of the gully, although I was able to keep my glass on him all the time. He came at a quiet trot straight towards me, springing lightly from stone to stone and only dropping down to the rough frozen ground when there was no other way. After travelling about a hundred yards in this way he turned aside at right angles and went a distance of about forty yards straight to a spot where a mass of heather grew in the cleft of a rock. Thrusting his head and half his body into the heather he began digging and presently pulled out something which he had concealed there and which he now proceeded to devour, holding it down with his paws. Having eaten it he sat down and licked his chops, then picked up the crumbs, so to speak, and sat down and licked his chops once more. Evidently the meat had not satisfied his hunger, for by-and-by he thrust himself into the clump and began digging again, but there was no more, and coming out he sat up again and with head inclining downwards remained for some moments in a dejected attitude, revolving things in his mind perhaps, and then, perhaps all at once remembering that he had another little hoard somewhere else, he started up and went off in a new direction with the same quiet trot as before, jumping lightly from stone to stone, and was soon lost to sight.

The raven I have spoken of was one of four that haunted this part of the coast, where they were very much hated by a pair of kestrels. One evening just before sunset I had a great surprise—when standing in a field half a mile from the sea talking to a farmer a flock of thirty-two ravens flew over our heads. It was impossible to make a mistake in this case, as the birds were flying quietly and low, passing directly over us at a height of scarcely forty yards. Undoubtedly they were strangers from a great distance, perhaps from the northern extremity of Scotland, and were making a tour round the whole island, but I had never heard of a migration of ravens into Cornwall in winter.

The two coldest days during the frost were the one on which I watched the fox and the day following. In the morning I had found the large window panes of my sitting-room thickly coated with a beautiful frost pattern, but the sky was clear and with the sun shining on the window and a big fire in the grate I thought it would soon be gone. It continued all day, although the fire never went out! The birds were now in desperate case: it appeared as if they had given up searching for food in despair, and were now idly waiting for a change or for the end, hunched up in any shelter they could find from the deadly north-east wind. The very daws were silent now, and dropped their wings like the others, as if they had not energy enough to fold them over their backs. Even the wren, that most vigorous little creature, the very type and embodiment of cheerfulness, had now too fallen into the universal misery, and came out of hiding languidly if it came at all, its feathers fluffed out and not a ghost of its sharp angry little voice to scold you with.

Towards evening on the second of the two worst days I went out to Zennor Hill to see the sun set from the top and watch the big furze and heath fires which were burning far and wide on the moor. On the slope of the hill I found a number of small companies of starlings, huddled together as usual by a hedge side, making no attempt to feed, there being nothing to be got from the iron earth; and as the sun declined they began to rise and fly away southwards to their roosting-place—a spot three or four miles inland, where a depression in the moor is covered with a dense growth of old furze mixed with blackthorn and brambles. Their miserable day was ended and numbers of small flocks of from a dozen to forty or fifty birds could now be seen against the sky, all directing their flight to the same point. It was a strangely slow and laborious flight, and many of the birds were going for the last time to their roost. From the summit where I tried to shelter myself from the fury of the wind among the large black masses of granite, the scene I looked upon was exceedingly desolate. The brown moor stretched away inland, lonely and dark, to the horizon. There was on all that expanse but one small object to arrest the sight—a frozen pool a couple of miles away which gleamed like grey glass in the level beams. Many heath fires were burning, one not above a mile from the hill and near enough for one to see the yellow flames running before the wind and leaping a dozen to twenty yards high. The sun seen through the vast clouds of dun smoke had the appearance of a globe of fiery red copper. After it had gone down and the earth began to darken the smoke took an intense orange colour from the flames, which seen against the pale blue sky gave a dreadful magnificence to the scene.

With this picture in my mind I went down the hill, chilled to the marrow, thinking of the birds asleep and occasionally disturbing one as I stumbled over the stones in the dark and picked my way among the black furze bushes. Indoors it was very comfortable, sitting by the fire, with the lighted lamp on the table and a book waiting to be read; then supper and a pipe, but through it all that strange and desolate aspect of nature remained persistently before my inner sight. I went to bed and lay soft and warm, covered with many blankets, but did not sleep; the wind increased in violence as the hours went on, making its doleful wailing and shrieking noises all round the house and causing the doors and windows to rattle in their frames. In spirit I was in it, out on the hillside where the birds were in their secret hiding-places, in the black furze and heath, in holes and crevices in the hedges, their little hearts beating more languidly each hour, their eyes glazing, until stiff and dead they dropped from their perches. And I was on the summit of the hill among the rude granite castles and sacred places of men who had their day on this earth thousands and thousands of years ago. Here there are great blocks and slabs of granite which have been artificially hollowed into basins—for what purpose, who shall say? The rain falls and fills them to the brim with crystal-clear water, and in summer the birds drink and bathe in these basins. But they were doubtless made for another, possibly for some dreadful, purpose. Perhaps they were filled from time to time with the blood of captive men sacrificed on the hill-top to some awful god of the ancient days. Now it seemed to me, out there in spirit on the hill, that the darkest imaginings of men—the blackest phantom or image of himself which he has sacrificed to—was not so dark as this dreadful unintelligible and unintelligent power that made us, in which we live and move and have our being.

It was this terrible aspect of nature, as I had seen it on that evening, which was uppermost in the mind of the race at an earlier stage of culture before man's cunning brain had found out so many inventions and created new and pleasant conditions for his own species. When animistic promptings survive in him he is now apt to personify nature in its milder beneficent aspects. Such personifications, fanciful and religious at the same time, are common in our imaginative writers, especially in the poets, but, when lying awake that night, I tried to recall the passages I had read just to contrast the brighter picture with that dark one in my mind, I could only remember one, in a prose writer, and it was this:

Nature is now at her evening prayers, kneeling before the red hills. On the steps of her great altar she is praying for a fair night for mariners at sea, for travellers in lonely deserts, for lambs on moors and for unfledged little birds in their nests. She appears to me as a Titanic woman, her robe of blue air spread to the outskirts of the heath; a veil white as an avalanche extends from her head to her feet with arabesques of lightning flame on its borders. Under her breasts is seen her purple zone, and through its blush shines the evening star. Her eyes are clear and deep as lakes, and are lifted and full of worship and tremble with the softness of love and the lustre of prayer.

Very curiously in this the only poetic passage I could recall the author's religion has mixed itself with the sense of a living and intelligent principle in nature—that which at times makes nature seem a *person* to us. The person may be interested in or indifferent to us, but is all-knowing and all-powerful and cannot be an intercessor. There is no doubt that this sense or feeling in us, when strong, is disturbing to the religious mind, producing as it does the notion of a something unknown and uncanny (probably the devil) in nature—something which is ever trying in all solitary places to seduce the soul from a jealous and watchful God. It was, I think, a religious poet and an American who wrote of the "dreadful wilderness of mind"—I read it when a boy:

> There is a wilderness more dark
> Than groves of fir on Huron's shore.

Many of us have just such visions of the person that nature is on occasions to us: a woman-Titan, beautiful female, the mother of men and of all life, all breathing sentient things, and of grass and flowers; a being in whom all beauty in the visible world and all sweetness and love and compassion in a mother's heart and in all hearts are concentrated and intensified. But it is a personification of a reclaimed and softened nature and of the soft conditions of life in which we are nursed. My vision of nature as a person that night had no softness or beauty in it and was not woman. Standing on the hills I saw him coming up from the illimitable moaning sea, riding on the blast as on a chariot, and he was himself wind and cloud and sea and land. He towered above the granite hills, blotting out the stars with his streaming hair which covered the heavens like a cloud. I saw his face, dark as granite, as he rose up before me and passed over the stony desolate hills, and his eyes gazing straight before him were like two immense round shields of grey ice and had no speculation in them. This indeed was to my mind the most dreadful thing, that this being, all-powerful and everlasting, creator and slayer of all things that live, of all beauty and sweetness and compassion, was himself without knowledge or thought or emotion, and that that which he had made and would unmake was without significance to him.

If there be nothing but this mechanical world, and if the pure materialist even in spite of his materialism should invent for himself or imagine a god, it would be such a one as I beheld on that windy night.

So passed the miserable darkling hours, "as I lay a-thynkinge," and saw no hope until I slept, and when I woke and the grey morning was come, the wind had fallen and the cold was not so intense.

The frost continued that day and the next, and although very cold with occasional storms of sleet and snow, it was getting milder all the time. The change was so gradual one could hardly feel it, but it had a great effect on the birds; they were recovering very rapidly, and on the morning of the 27th, when the ground had once more grown soft except in shady places, my birds did not turn up at feeding-time in the morning: they were back in the fields getting their natural food, which no doubt tasted best after their long abstinence. It was a pleasure to go out again to see the thrush standing up stiff and alert on the green turf in the old way, and the speckled starlings scattered about and once more busily prodding the turf. The daws rose up with the old insolent ring in their clamouring voices, and the wren was himself again, briskly hopping out of his hiding-place in the stones for a moment or two just to fling that sharp little note of indignation at you for disturbing him—"Go away—mind your own business!"

The mortality had undoubtedly been very great, but a majority of the birds died in the night-time, dropping from their perches in the close bushes and dying in holes in the hedges, where their bodies remained hidden. But they had died in the daytime too, and I found their remains all about the fields, mostly starlings, but dead redwings and thrushes were also plentiful.

A NATIVE NATURALIST

THE Towans, as the sandhills or dunes on the north-east side of St. Ives Bay are called—that barren place mentioned in the last chapter where a horde of fugitive thrushes found snails enough to save them from starving—is a curiously attractive bit of country. It is plainly visible from St. Ives, looking east over the water—a stretch of yellow sands where the Hayle River empties itself in the bay, and, behind it, a grey-green desert of hummocky or hilly earth, where the hills are like huge broken waves in "fluctuation fixed." And in a sense they are waves, formed of sand which the ocean brings out of its depths and exposes at low water, to be swept up by the everlasting winds and heaped in hills along the sea-front; and no sooner are the hills built than the wind unbuilds them again, carrying the yellow dust further inland to build other hills and yet others, burying the green farm-lands and houses and entire villages in their desolating progress. This, they say, was the state of things no longer ago than the eighteenth century, when some wise person discovered or remembered that Nature herself has a remedy for this evil, a means of staying the wind-blown sands in their march. The common sea rush, *Psamma arenaria,* the long coarse grass which grows on the sand by the sea, was introduced—the roots or seed, I do not know which; and it grew and spread, and in a little while took complete possession of all that desolate strip of land, clothing the deep hollows and wave-like hills to their summits with its pale, sere looking, grey-green tussocks. As you walk there, when the wind blows from the sea, the fine, dry, invisible particles rain on your face and sting your eyes; but all this travelling sand comes from the beach and can do no harm, for where it falls it must lie and serve as food for the conquering sea rush. If you examine the earth you will find it bound down with a matting of tough roots and rootlets, and that in the spaces between the tussocks the decaying rush has formed a thin mould and is covered with mosses and lichens, and in many places with a turf as on the chalk downs.

The Towans occupy the ground on both sides of the estuary. On the south side is the ancient village of Lelant, once threatened with destruction by the shifting sands; now the square old church tower, as you approach it from St. Ives, is seen standing bravely above the rush-grown hills and hummocks made harmless for ever. On the north side of the estuary is Hayle, a small decayed town, and the ancient village and church of Phillack, and behind the village to the sea and on either hand miles upon miles of towans. There is a ferry at Lelant, and the ferryman has his little ramshackle hut at the foot of a sandhill, a little below the church, and here I often came to be rowed over to the other side, where it was wilder and more solitary. There I could spend hours at a stretch without seeing a human being or hearing any sound of human life. From the top of a high towan I could get a fine view of the bay, with St. Ives' little town and rocky island on the further side; while looking along the coastline on the right hand, the white tower of Godrevy Light house on its rock was seen at the end of the bay, and beyond it the blue Atlantic. Coming down from my look-out all the wide exhilarating prospect would vanish—ocean and bay and distant town, with cliffs and hills—and I would be in another world, walking on the soft sand and moss in hollow places among the tall sere rushes with their old bleached seed-spikes. "They have no song, the sedges dry," sings the poet, but in his heart, he adds, they touched a string and for him they had a song. So it was with these dry rushes; they touched a string in me, and that low, rustling, sibilant sound, and mysterious whispering which the wind made in them, was to me a song. There was not even a bird voice to break the silence, except when I disturbed a meadow pipit and it rose and flew to this side and that in its usual uncertain way, uttering its sharp, thin, melancholy note of alarm—a sound which serves to intensify the feeling of wildness and to give an expression to earth in lonely desert places.

In my visits to the Towans I had a double motive and pleasure: one in communing with nature in that "empty and solitary place," the other in talking with the ferryman who took me to and fro across the river: he was a native of the place, a pure Cornishman in appearance and disposition, and a naturalist. I do not say a "born naturalist" because I fancy we are most of us that, and yet the countryman who is a naturalist is a rarity. As a rule, what he knows about nature and wild life is the little that survives in his memory of all he learnt in his boyhood. He learns a good deal then, when the mind is fresh, the senses keen and the ancient hunting and exploring instincts most active. "In woods and wilds the naked savage ran," and the civilised boy still preserves the old tradition, and as he runs he picks up a good deal of knowledge which will be of no use to him. If he is a country boy of the labouring class he no sooner arrives at an age to leave school and idling and do something for a living than the change begins—a change which is like a metamorphosis. However small a part he is called on to fill, though he be but a carter's boy, it serves to open a new prospect to his mind, and to give him a new and absorbing interest in life. His work is the most important thing in the world: he ponders on it, and on the money it brings him; on the tremendous question of food and clothing and shelter; and by-and-by on love and marriage and children to follow; on the struggle to live and the great difference that a shilling or two more or less per week will be to him. One effect of all this is to make the interests and occupations of his early years appear trivial; his days with wild nature were all idle and useless and the knowledge of animal life he acquired of as little consequence as that of the old boyish games. The country youth would perhaps be astonished if he could be conscious of the change going on in him, or if someone were to tell him that the mental images of things seen and heard in nature will soon grow dim and eventually fade out of his mind. It is really surprising to find how far this dimming and obliterating process will go; for here (let us say) is a man whose whole life is passed amidst the same rural scenes, who has seen and heard the same bird forms and sounds from infancy, who knew them all as intimately as he knew his mother's face and voice in his early years, and yet he has ceased to know them! All because he has not renewed or refreshed the early images; because his mind has been occupied with other things exclusively, and his faculty of observation, with regard to nature at all events, has practically ceased to exist.

An amusing instance of this state of mind occurs to me here. I was staying in a small rustic village in the cottage of one of the most interesting men I have met. He was a working man, better educated than most of his class, and at the age of sixty-five had saved enough to buy a plot of ground and build himself a little house with his own hands in which to spend the remnant of his life without further labour. But he was of an active mind and an enthusiast inflamed with one great idea and hope, which was to raise the people of his own class to a better position and a higher life— morally and intellectually—to make them, in fact, as sober, righteous, independent and wise as he was himself. And as he was a man of character and courage, and gifted with a kind of eloquence, he had come to be very widely known and greatly respected; he had even been led to fight a hard fight in a populous borough as a Labour candidate for Parliament. He had lost but was not in the least soured by defeat and was still a leader of men, a sort of guide, philosopher and friend to very many of his own class, especially in matters political Finally, he was a man of a noble presence, large and powerfully built, with a genial open countenance and a magnificent white beard—a sort of Walt Whitman both in appearance and temper of mind, his love of humanity, his tolerance and above all his unshakable faith in a glorious democracy.

All this about my leader of working men has nothing to do with the subject under discussion, but I could not resist the temptation of giving a portrait of the man.

One bright spring day I was with him, pacing his garden walk, discussing a variety of important matters relating to man's spiritual nature, and so forth, when by-and-by we drifted into other themes—wild nature, and then wild bird life. "There is," he said, "one curious thing about birds in which they differ from other creatures and which makes them a little more puzzling to a man with just the ordinary knowledge of nature. They have wings to carry them about and they roam from place to place, so that at any moment a man may be confronted with a bird of a perfectly unfamiliar appearance. Or he may hear a cry or song which he has never heard before, and in such a case he can only say that the bird must be a stranger in that locality—a wanderer from some distant place. But one would always like to know what the bird is; it adds to the interest, and I have very often wished when seeing or hearing some such strange bird that some one like yourself, with an intimate knowledge of all the species in our country, had been with me to satisfy my curiosity."

Just as he was finishing a chaffinch flew down and vanished into the dense foliage of a young horse-chestnut tree growing a dozen yards from where we stood, and no sooner had it come down than it burst out in its familiar loud ringing lyric.

He started round and held up his hand. "There!" he exclaimed when the bird ended his song. "A case in point! Now can you tell me what bird was that?"

"A chaffinch," I said.

He looked sharply, almost resentfully, at me, thinking it a poor joke on my part, and when I smiled at his expression he was more put out than ever. But I could not help admiring him as he stood there staring into my face. He had put down his spade when our talk began; his coat was off, his cloudy old brown waistcoat unbuttoned, his blue cotton shirt-sleeves rolled up to the elbows, his hands and arms smeared with dried clay—a grand figure of a man with the white beard mixed with a little red falling to his waist, his grey old shapeless felt hat thrust back on his head and his long hair down to his shoulders.

He assured me with dignity that if there was a bird he was familiar with it was the chaffinch, that as a person born and bred in the country he could not make a mistake about such a bird. Nevertheless, I returned, the bird we had heard was a chaffinch, and familiar as he was with such a bird he could not pit his knowledge against mine in such a case. He assented but still felt dissatisfied. "You will allow, I suppose," he said, "that there are great differences in individual singers and that some one bird may be so different from the generality as to deceive one who is not an ornithologist as to its species."

He was right there, I said, and that consoled him, and he concluded that this particular bird had uttered an unusual sort of song which no person, not a trained naturalist, would have identified as that of a chaffinch.

It was not so, but I let it pass, and he was glad to get back to other higher subjects where he was, so to speak, on his native heath and could be my guide.

This may appear an extreme case: I do not think so; I have conversed about the creatures with too many rustics and country people of all denominations to think it anything out of the common—scores and hundreds of rustics all over the country, and if I want to hear something fresh and interesting I go to the boy and not to his stolid father, or hoary-headed less stolid grandfather, who have both pretty well forgotten all they once knew.

Of course there are exceptions, especially among gamekeepers, although in a majority of cases their observation is of that baser kind which concerns itself solely with the things that profit. But there is also the nobler kind of observer, the one in a thousand whose keen boyish interest in all living things is not lost when he is called on to take a part in the serious business of life. Ceasing to be a boy he does not put away this boyish thing, this secret delight in nature which others outlive. It is in him like the memory of a first love, the image of a vanished form, which endures in the mind to extreme old age and outlasts and has a lustre beyond all others. It is this surviving feeling of the boy which makes the native naturalist, the man with keen observant eye and retentive memory; and however illiterate he may be, or unsocial in disposition, or uncouth or repellent in manners, it is always a delight to meet him, to conquer his rudeness or reserve and to listen to the strange experiences garnered in his memory.

In the chapter on Cornish imagination something was said about the actions of animals, even of those we are most familiar with, which come as a great surprise, and I gave an account of one—an incident I witnessed of a rock pipit which, caught by a violent gust of wind just at the moment when its wings being set for the gliding descent to earth could not be used to resist the current, was blown away into the midst of a band of hovering herring gulls and very nearly lost its life. One knows that one will never witness just such an incident again, but there will be others equally unexpected and strange for the watcher. In the course of this book I have related a few: one of a gannet falling from a great height like a stone into the sea just by the side of a herring gull floating on the surface, and one of a fox, standing like a carved figure on a big rock, savagely attacked by a raven and refusing to be driven from its stand.

Here I cannot resist the temptation to introduce an incident of this kind, but far more wonderful than any one I have related in this or any other book, which was witnessed not by a naturalist but an artist, my friend Mr. R. H. Carter, of the Land's End. He was with his friend, the late Rev. F. C. Jackson, Rector of Stanmore, who used to take his holidays in West Cornwall and was himself something of an artist. They were sketching one day on the huge cliffs of Tol-Pedn-Penwith, near the Land's End, when Mr. Carter noticed that some animal had been recently scratching the earth at the foot of a huge pile of rocks near where he was sitting. There was a large hollow place under the rock into which one could see, as there was an opening on a level with the ground on one side, and it struck him that a badger had taken refuge in this cavity, and had been obliged to scratch a little earth away to squeeze his body in. He called his companion's attention to it, and getting down on the turf and lying flat so as to bring their eyes on to a level with the floor they gazed into the cavity. They could see no animal, but the light was dim inside, and Mr. Jackson proceeded to twist up half a dozen wax matches into a small compact ball, which he lighted and then carefully pushed in right to the middle of the hollow space. The burning wax made a good light, but still they could see no creature, only at one side, a foot or so from the light, there was a dark patch which they could not make out; it was, they imagined, a hole in the rock which showed black. Presently, as they gazed in, still trying to penetrate into that dark hole with their sight, a paw was seen to emerge and move towards the light, until the whole foreleg of a badger was revealed; then the paw scraped up a little loose soil from the floor and carefully drew or jerked it over the burning ball of wax and put the light out.

They had both witnessed the whole action, and by-and-by with a long stick or pole they succeeded in ousting the badger from his niche in the little cave. Had they not done so the sceptical reader might have said that what they had seen was an illusion—that they were looking for a badger and expecting to see one and had badger on the brain, so to speak; and by-and-by when a slight moving shadow caused by the flickering flame made its appearance it took the form of a badger's paw and leg in their sight, and when the flame expired they imagined that the illusory paw had extinguished it. I dare say that if such an incident had been related by the Canadian, Charles Roberts, or by any of the writers of the "new or romantic school" of natural history in America, it would be set down by most readers as an unusually wild invention of the author.

The ferryman had no such wonderful story to tell when we compared notes, and I intend here to relate only a few of the curious incidents he had witnessed, and this mainly for a purpose of my own. They were mostly little tragedies.

One summer day when he was out in his boat fishing for pollack at his favourite ground a mile or two beyond the Godrevy Lighthouse he noticed three guillemots near him, one old bird with its half-grown young one, and a second young bird which accompanied the others but kept at a little distance from them. This young guillemot had doubtless been lost or left by its parents. There was no other bird in sight except a great black-backed gull, flying idly about, now making a wide circle and occasionally dropping on to the water to examine some small floating object, then flying off again. He appeared to pay no attention to the guillemots, nor they to him, and it therefore came as a great surprise when all at once in passing over the three birds he dropped down upon the second young guillemot and seized it before it had time to dive. The captive struggled in vain, sending forth its shrill cries for help far and wide over the still sea, while the great gull, sitting on the surface, proceeded in a leisurely manner to despatch and then devour his victim, tearing it to pieces with his big powerful yellow beak.

He told me of several other little tragedies of the kind which he had witnessed with surprise, one of a curlew which at the moment of flying past him was suddenly chased by a sparrow-hawk and pressed so hard that it dashed down to the beach, where it was instantly grappled. The ferryman made all haste to the spot, and the hawk flew off at his approach, leaving the curlew dead and bleeding on the sands. He picked it up and took it home to eat it himself. But of all these cases the one of the great black-backed gull impressed him the most on account of the

casual way in which it came about, just as if the gull had been taken by
a sudden impulse to drop upon and slaughter the young guillemot. Such
an incident serves to show how perilous a world the wild creature exists
in and on how small a matter its safety often depends, and it also gives the
idea of an almost uncanny intelligence in the birds that live by violence.
No doubt the gull was tempted to fall on that young bird solely because
of its keeping a little apart from the other two, because it had no parent
of its own to protect it.

The rocks to the north of St. Ives Bay are an ancient haunt of the
common seal, one of the few colonies of this animal now left on the
south coast of Britain. The ferryman was one day fishing in his boat at
this point close to the mouth of that vast cavern in the rocks where the
seals have their home, when a loud barking cry or roar made him jump
in his boat, and looking round he caught sight of a seal thrusting his head
and half his body out of the water with a conger about seven to eight
feet long fastened to his ear. The blood was streaming from the seal's head
and he was trying to shake his enemy off and at the same time turning
round and round in his efforts to bite the conger; but the black serpentine
body wriggled and floated out of his reach, and in a very few moments
they went down. Again and again they rose, the seal coming out each
time with the same savage cry, shaking himself and biting, the conger still
holding on with bull-dog tenacity. But on the last occasion there was no
cry and commotion; the conger had lost his hold and the seal had him by
the middle of the body in his jaws. On coming up he swam quietly to the
sloping rock close by, and half in, half out of the water began tearing up
and devouring his victim, the blood still running from his own head.

He had another seal story which interested me even more than the last,
since the chief actor and conqueror in this instance was the nobler animal
man, the seal being the victim.

In the early autumn of 1907 there were mighty winds on this coast,
with tremendous seas and very high tides, which made it impossible to
use the ferry; but when the weather moderated and the ferryman took
to his boat once more he came upon a young seal, which had, no doubt,
taken refuge in the Hayle estuary and was lost from its parents. The days
went by and it did not leave the river: the mother seal had not found
it, and apparently the poor young thing had no sure instinct to guide
it across St. Ives Bay to the seal caverns in the cliffs to the north of the
lighthouse, which was probably its birthplace. And probably finding itself
very lonely in the estuary it came by-and-by to look on the man in the
boat, who was always there, as a sort of companion—perhaps as a seal of

curious habits, which looked a little like an adult seal, but progressed in a somewhat different manner, keeping always to the surface of the water and swimming with the aid of two long wing-like fins. But it appeared to be a good-natured seal! and always regarded the orphaned youngster with a mild and welcoming expression. First it watched the ferry-man from a little distance, then approached him every time he appeared, then began to follow, coming nearer and nearer, and would swim behind the boat, quite close, just as a spaniel or other water-loving dog will swim after its master's boat.

This was a delightful experience to the ferryman, and the sight of the dog-like creature swimming after the boat was also an entertainment to the passengers and a cause of surprise to many. But there was nothing remarkable in its action; the seal, like the dog, is a social creature; it is well known that he readily grows tame towards, and even attached to, the human beings he is accustomed to see who do not persecute him. The old Cornish author, Borlase, refers to this character of the seal, which he classes with his "Quadruped Reptiles," in the following quaint passage:

> Whether it is delighted with music or any land voice, or whether it is to alleviate the toil of swimming, it shows itself almost wholly above the water frequently, or near the shore. Add to this that the great docility of the creature (little short of that of the human species) and his being so easily trained to be familiar with and obedient to man, may make us with some grounds conclude, that this is the creature to which imagination has given the shape of half-fish, half-man, a shape nowhere else to be found.

The estuary attracts a good number of wild fowl, duck and shore birds, in winter, and as a consequence is much frequented by sportsmen. One day the ferryman took one of these gentlemen, a visitor from a distance, across the river, and was not half way over before the seal appeared as usual and with its head well up swam after the boat, and gaining quickly on it was soon not more than an oar's length from the stern. The ferryman, looking back, was watching it, and by-and-by, thinking it would be a pleasant surprise to the other, he remarked, "My baby seal is just behind you, coming after us." The other looked around, and instantly, before the boatman could cry out or even divine his intention, threw up his gun and fired, and the brains of the young seal were scattered on the water. "You have killed my pet seal—the animal I loved best," the boatman cried, and the other was surprised and expressed regret. He wished he had known it was a pet seal; he wouldn't have killed it, no, not for anything, if he had only known. And why had he not been warned? and so on, until he stepped out of the boat and went his way with his gun.

He had not been warned because in spite of all the ferryman had seen of sportsmen and their ways he never imagined that anyone would have done so brutal a thing or that the murderous shot would have been fired so quickly.

He also told me about an osprey which appeared one autumn at the estuary. It was the first bird of its species he had ever seen, and when it first appeared, flying high in the air and hovering directly over his hut where he kept a number of fowls and turkeys, he became alarmed for their safety, thinking it was a kite or other large destructive hawk. By-and-by the strange bird sailed away and began circling above the water, coming lower down, then after hovering at one spot like a kestrel for some moments he saw it drop into the water and rise with a good-sized fish in its talons. Then he knew that the strange big hawk was the famous osprey.

For some days it displayed its magnificent powers to all who came to the water-side, exciting a great deal of interest; then one of the sporting gentle men succeeded in getting a shot at it and wounding it badly. But it did not drop; it was watched flying laboriously away over the moor until out of sight and was never seen again.

Another season he had a great northern diver in the river, and this bird after a week or ten days lost its wildness and took no notice of the ferryman, although he sometimes rowed his boat to within forty yards of it to watch its movements when it was fishing. The sportsmen he ferried across wanted to shoot the diver, but he prevented them. Then one gentleman told him that he would hire a boat and go out and shoot it, in spite of him. He said that a bird so destructive to fish should not be allowed to live in the river. The ferryman said he would prove to him that the diver was doing no harm, and rowing him out to where the bird was diving at its usual feeding-ground they watched, and presently saw it come up with a small green crab in its beak. The sportsman was convinced that the bird was not taking fish, and gave his promise that he would not shoot it. However, a day or two later it was shot at by one of the sports men and badly wounded in the side, and from that time the sight of it was a constant pain to him as it moved continually round and round in a circle when attempting to swim and was hardly able to dive. Finally he took his gun and put it out of its misery.

The young seal, the osprey, the great northern diver were but a few of the creatures he told me of, which, when living, were a source of delight to everyone who watched them, whose lives had been wantonly taken in the estuary by gentlemen sportsmen. Stories equally sad and shocking were told me by other lovers of nature and observers of wild life at other points on the coast, of how every rare and beautiful species, every owl, buzzard, harrier, chough, hoopoe and many other species, had been slaughtered by men who call themselves sportsmen and gentlemen. How is one to explain such a thing—this base destructive passion—unless it be that the gentleman, like the gamekeeper, cannot escape the reflex effect on his mind of the gun in his hand? He too has grown incapable of pleasure in any rare or noble or beautiful form of life until he has it in his hands—until he has exercised his awful power and blotted out its existence. And how hard of heart the exercise has made him!

One afternoon at Wells-by-the-Sea I entered into conversation with a sportsman I found sitting on a grassy slope, where he was waiting for the wild geese which would come in by-and-by from feeding to roost on the sand-spit outside. He was, physically, a very fine fellow in his prime, tall, athletic-looking, with a handsome typical English face of that hard colour which comes of an open-air life, with the hard keen eyes so often seen in the sportsman. Talking with him I discovered that he was also a man of culture, a great traveller, a reader and a collector of rare and costly books on certain subjects, especially on the forms of sport he loved best. It was impossible for me not to admire him as he sat there reclining idly on his rug, thrown on the green slope, smoking his pipe, his gun lying across his knees, his big black curly-haired retriever stretched out at his side. And at intervals, as we talked, a little meadow pipit, the only other living creature near us, flitted out of the grass and, rising to a height of twenty or thirty feet, hovered over the still water beneath, as if to get a better view of us, to find out what we were doing there; and as it hovered before us it emitted those sharp, sorrowful little call-notes which have such a charm for me. And every time the small bird rose and hovered before us the dog raised his head and watched it excitedly, then looked up into his master's face. Then the little thing with an anxious mind would drop back on the turf again and go on seeking its food as before, so near to us that we could distinctly see its bright eyes and thin little pale brown legs and all the markings and shadings of its pretty winter plumage—the olive-browns and dull blacks, the whites and the cream faintly tinged with buff on the striped breast.

By-and-by I got up and strolled away to the dunes on the sea-front, and when I had gone about seventy or eighty yards a shot rang out behind me. Glancing back I saw that the sportsman had also got up and was now walking to a point among the dunes where he had planned to lie in wait for the geese. The retriever was some distance behind, playing with something; and then, instead of following his master, he came on to me, and seeing that he was carrying something I stooped down and drew it from his mouth. It was the titling—the little meadow pipit; its anxious little question and challenge had been answered with an idle charge of shot when it flew up and hovered before the man with a gun.

I suppose that his motive, if he had one, was to give his dog a few minutes' amusement in retrieving the shattered little bird from the water and in playing with and carrying it. But if I had gone to him and demanded to know why he had taken that happy little life, which was sacred to me, I think his answer, if he had condescended to make one, would have been very contemptuous—I think he would have said that he perceived me to be a sentimentalist and that he declined to say anything to a person of that sort.

There are not, I imagine, many men of so fine a temper of mind as to escape this hardening effect of the gun in the hand.

In conclusion of this chapter I will go back to the subject of the Cornish seals of that small surviving colony which has its ancestral home in the caves outside the Bay of St. Ives. Sportsmen occasionally shoot them just for the pleasure of the thing, but the fishermen of St. Ives do not consider that they suffer any injury from the animals and have consequently refrained from persecuting them. Unhappily they are now threatened with extermination from a new quarter: the students at the Camborne Mining School have recently found out a new and pleasant pastime, which is to seat themselves with rifle or fowling-piece on the cliff and watch for the appearance of a brown head above the water below of a seal going out of or coming in to the caves, and letting fly at it. When they hit the seal it sinks and is seen no more, but the animal is not wanted, the object is to shoot it, and this accomplished the sportsman goes back happy and proud at his success in having murdered so large and human-like a creature.

THE COMING OF SPRING

AFTER the frost described two chapters back, the change to the normal winter temperature was so great as to make it seem like spring before the end of January. When spring does come to England, known to all by many welcome signs, it makes but a very slight difference in this West Cornwall district and is hardly recognised. For more than half the year, from October to May, it is comparatively a verdureless and flowerless land, dark with furze and grey with rocks and heather, splashed with brown-red of dead bracken. Not till the end of May will the bracken live again and make the rough wilderness green, and not till July will the dead-looking heath have its flush of purple colour. Nevertheless, from autumn onwards the sense of spring in the earth is never long absent. It rains and rains; sea-mists come up and blot out the sight of all things, and the wind raves everlastingly, and, finally, there may be a spell of frost or a fall of snow; but through it all, at very frequent intervals, the subtle influence, the "ethereal mildness," makes itself felt. It is as if the sweet season had never really forsaken this end of all the land, following the receding sun, but rather as if it had retired with the adder and the mother bumble-bee into some secret hiding-place to sleep a little while and wake as often as the rain ceased and the wind grew still to steal forth and give a mysterious gladness to the air. It is felt even more by the wild creatures than by man, and I think that John Cocking is one of the first to show it, for by mid-January he has got himself a curly crest and a new spirit.

John Cocking is the local name of the shag, the commonest species of cormorant on this coast, a big, heavy, ungainly-looking creature, the ugliest fowl in Britain, half bird and half reptile in appearance on the water, where he spends half his time greedily devouring fish and the other half sitting on the rocks digesting his food and airing his wings. It is hard to imagine any softening or beautifying change in such a being, and indeed the only alteration to be observed in him at first is that he begins to pay some attention to his fellow-shags and to find out occasion to quarrel with them. I watched the behaviour of one, a tyrant and hooligan, at Gurnard's Head, at a spot where a mass of rocks overlooking the sea has one perfectly flat stone on the top. This stone was a favourite standing-place of the shags on account of its position and flat surface, and it afforded space enough to accommodate a score or more birds. The bird I watched had placed himself in the centre of the flat rock and would not allow another to share it with him. At intervals of a few minutes a cormorant coming up from the sea would settle on it, as he had always or for a long time been accustomed to do, whereupon the John Cocking in possession would twist his snaky head round and glare at him with his malignant emerald-green eyes. If this produced no effect he would open wide his beak and dart his head out towards the intruder just as an irritated adder lunges at you when you are out of his reach. Then, if the new comer still refused to quit, he would pull himself up erect and hurl his heavy body against the other and send him flying off the rock. The ejected one would then either fly away or find himself a place on the sloping rock among the nine or ten others who had been treated in the same way. Meanwhile the ruffian himself would go back to the middle of the stone platform, holding his tail stuck up vertically like a staff, and turn himself about this way and that as if asking the whole company if there was any other Johnny there who would like to try conclusions with him.

The softening of the ugly bird comes a little later when the hooligan has got a mate and both are half beside themselves with joy, which they express by rubbing their snaky necks together, crossing and see-sawing them, first on one side then the other, like knife and steel in the butcher's hands. When the nesting-site has been chosen, John Cocking is seen at his best, playing the attentive young husband; he visits her twenty times an hour, always with some thing in his beak, a bit of seaweed or a stick, just because he must give her something, and she takes it from him and bows this way and that and puts it down and takes it up again, and out of her overflowing affection gives it back to him—"Dear, you must not be so generous!" And he flies away with it again just to have an excuse to fly back the next minute and insist on her accepting it. The great change, greater even than his new charming manner towards his mate, is in his flight on quitting the nesting-place: he flies and returns, and passes and repasses before her, and alights on the rock for a moment and then off again—all to exhibit his grace, his imitation of the love-flight of the cushat and turtle-dove. The curious thing is that so heavy and ungainly a creature, with such a laboured flight at other times, does succeed fairly well, as if that new fire in him had made him lighter, more volatile and like the white-winged birds about him.

The cormorants are the earliest breeders, excepting the ravens, now so much persecuted by the injurious idiots and Philistines who call themselves collectors and naturalists that they rarely succeed in rearing their young; and the next to follow are the herring gulls. The gull fixes on a site for his nest, but long before building begins he appears anxious to let all his neighbours know that this particular spot is his very own and that he looks on their approach with jealous eyes. Not green eyes like the cormorant's, but of a very pure luminous yellow like the vivid eyes of a harrier hawk, or some brilliant yellow gem, or like the glazed petal of a buttercup lit by a sun beam. His gull neighbours respect his rights, but the jackdaws mock at his feeling of proprietorship and amuse themselves very much at his expense.

One day I watched a pair of gulls on a rock they had recently taken possession of—a large mass of granite thrust out from the cliff over the sea. The female was reposing at the spot where it was intended the nest should be, while the male kept guard, walking proudly about on his little domain, now turning an eye up to watch the birds flying overhead, then stooping to pick up a pebble to hold it a few moments in his bill and drop it again, and then marching up to his mate, whereupon they would open wide their yellow beaks, stretch out their necks and join their voices in a loud triumphant chant. "Here we are," he appeared to be saying, "established on our own rock, which belongs exclusively to us with every thing on it, even to the smallest pebble and to every leaf and flower of the thrift and sea-campion growing on it. Not a bird of them all will venture to alight on this rock. Come now, stand up and let us shout together!"

And shout they did, their loudest, and in the middle of their shouting performance a jackdaw, detaching himself from a company of thirty or forty birds wheeling about overhead, dropped plump down on to the rock. Instantly the gull dashed at and drove him away, but no sooner was he back on his rock than he found the daw back too, and had to hunt him away again, and then again to the ninth time. And at last when he had been mocked nine times he became furious and set himself to give the insolent daw a lesson he would not forget: over the sea and land and along the face of the cliff he chased him, and up into the sky they rose and down again, the daw at his greatest speed, the pursuer screaming with wrath close behind him, but he could not catch or hurt him, and at last giving up the chase returned to alight once more on his rock. But the daw had followed him back, and no sooner had the gull folded his wings than down on the rock he dropped once more and sat there, a picture of impudence, eyeing the other's movements with his little white mocking eyes. What will happen now? I asked myself. But the gull was not going to be made a fool of any more; he put up with the insult, and after two or three minutes, finding he was to have no more fun, the daw flew off to rejoin his companions.

Sea-birds, visible from the headlands, are common enough throughout the cold season, but after mid-winter their numbers increase, until at last you may see the travellers passing by in small flocks of a dozen to a hundred or even two hundred birds, almost every day and often all day long, flock succeeding flock as if they were all keeping in a line—puffins, razorbills, guillemots—flying low on rapidly-beating wings, their bodies showing black and white just above the rough surface of the sea. More interesting than these in appearance are those dusky-winged swifts of the ocean, the shearwaters, travellers the same way, not in flocks but singly and in twos and threes and sometimes as many as half a dozen, all keeping wide apart, searching the sea as they go, moving very swiftly above the water in a series of wide curves looking like shadows of birds passing, invisible, far up in the sky. Sometimes they seemed like shadows, and sometimes I imagined them to be the ghosts of those pelagic birds which had recently died in all the seas which flow round the world, travelling by some way mysteriously known to them to their ultimate bourne in the furthest north, beyond the illimitable fields of ice where, according to Courthope, dead birds have their paradise.

While this migration is visibly going on at sea another is in progress all over the land which is not seen or not noticed, and this is the departure of visitants from the northern parts of Britain which have been wintering in Cornwall. From day to day their numbers diminish imperceptibly— first field-fares and redwings; then starlings, thrushes, larks, pipits, wagtails and some other species which come in smaller numbers. By the end of February or quite early in March the winter visitors, British and foreign, have all slipped quietly away, their east ward movement unmarked, and still no new bird from oversea has come to take their place. Then, one day in March when the sun shines, as you stroll by the sea, suddenly a flash of white comes before you at a distance of forty or fifty yards and you see your first wheat ear, or whitaker as the natives call him, back in his old home among the rocks. And as he is the first to come you think him the most beautiful bird in the world in his chaste and delicate dress of black and white and buff and clear blue-grey. And so when you first hear him uttering his wild brief warble, as he flutters in the air in appearance a great black and white butterfly, you think that no sound can compare with it in exquisite purity, and sweetness.

Away from the sea you will hear no spring bird; the only songs are of the resident species which you have heard at intervals throughout the winter—robin and wren and dunnock and lark and corn bunting. The only new song—if song it may be called—is not uttered by a bird at all, although it often has a curiously bird-like musical tinkle. You begin to hear it as you ramble among the furze thickets in the neighbourhood of some hidden stream—a succession of chirping and croaking sounds in various keys, and sounds like the craking of corncrakes, and at intervals the little musical sounds as of birds and of running water. The frogs are having their grand annual carnival, and when seen congregated at the water-courses, it is strange to think they should be so abundant in this stony district overgrown with harsh furze, ling and bracken. You have perhaps spent months in the place without seeing a frog, now following the stream you could count hundreds at their revels in the water, brown and olive frogs, clay colour, yellow and old gold, and some strangely marked with black and brown on a pale ground. These congregations which begin to form before March are continued until May.

Adders, seen occasionally on warm days in February, are common enough in March and April if one knows how to find them. Here, at two spots within half a mile of each other, I found two of the most singular and beautifully coloured adders I had ever seen. One was of so pale a grey in its ground colour as to appear white at a little distance; the other was perfectly white, the zigzag band intensely black with a narrow border of delicate buff. I turned him over expecting to find some curious variation in the colour of the belly, and was disappointed to find it the usual dark blue; but I was so charmed with this rare Dominican adder that I kept it half an hour, carrying it to a piece of level green turf for the pleasure of watching the sinuous movements of so strange a serpent over the ground before I finally let it go into hiding among the bushes.

After you have seen and heard the wheatears you begin to listen in the furze- and thorn-grown bottoms for that bright, airy, tender, running, rippling little melody of the willow-wren, which should come next, and is so universal in England, and it will surprise you to hear the chiffchaff before him, for in this treeless district the species so abundant everywhere else is comparatively rare, while the local chiffchaff is exceedingly common.

Before the earliest summer migrants are heard some of the resident species are breeding, not only on the cliffs, but the small birds in the bushes—thrushes, blackbirds, dunnocks, wrens and others. I was surprised to find that clothes-drying was a very serious trouble to these bush-breeders where there are no trees. Monday is washing-day at the farms and cottages, and it is usual to use the stone hedges covered with their luxuriant crop of furze as a drying-place. Looking over the land from some elevated place you see the gleam of white linen far and near as, of hedges covered with snow. Passing one of these hedges one evening I found a gathering of about a dozen blackbirds in a state of great excitement, hopping and flying up and down, chuckling and screaming before the white sheets and counterpanes covering some of the large round bushes. Poor birds! it was late in the day and they were getting desperate, since if these hateful white coverings were not removed soon, so as to let them return to their nests, their eggs would be chilled beyond hope. Some of the birds care as little for the covering sheet as rooks and jackdaws do for the grotesque imitations of a human figure set up in the ploughed fields to frighten them. A woman in one of the cottages told me that once when going round among the furze bushes where her things were drying she noticed a dunnock slip out from under a sheet and fly away. She lifted the sheet and found a nest with fledglings in it close to the top of the bush. "Why, gracious me!" she exclaimed, "perhaps been covering their dear little nesties with my washing without ever knowing such a thing. I'll just have a look at the other bushes." And at the very next bush on peering under the cloth spread over it she spied a dunnock sitting on its nest—sitting, she soon found, on five lovely little blue eggs! In the evening when the family were having tea she told them about it, and immediately her boys began to tease her to tell them where the nest was, and after a good deal of talk and solemn promise on the part of the boys that they would not take nor even touch one of the little blue eggs, and many warnings on her side that they would have the rope's end if they ever dared to do such a cruel thing, she led the way to the bush and allowed them all to have a good look at the nest and the five little gems of blue colour lying in it. But from that day she had no peace, for now her bad boys had got a means of coercing her, and she had to let them stay away from school and go where and do what they liked and to give them bread and butter and pasties at all hours of the day and whatever they asked for; for if she refused them anything they would say, "Then we'll go and get the eggs out of the hedge-sparrow's nest"; nor could she punish them for anything they did for the same reason. It was only when the blue eggs hatched and the young birds were safely reared that she got the upper hand in her house once more. Poor, anxious, thin, shrill-voiced woman, fighting for a small bird with her rough sons, her husband standing silent by listening with amused contempt to the dispute; for he too had been a boy, and was not the harrying of birds a boy's proper pastime? But she was one of the few who made it possible for me to live with and not hate my fellow-creatures even in these habitations of cruelty.

In conclusion of this chapter I will relate two other little incidents of this kind which show that the spirit of mercy is not wholly dead. A pair of pied wagtails were constantly seen at a stone quarry near a village I stayed at, and as they appeared very tame I spoke to the quarrymen about them. They said the birds had lived there, winter and summer, five years, and bred every spring in a hole among the stones at the side of the quarry. They were as tame as chickens and came for crumbs every day at dinner time, and when it was raining and the men had to take shelter in their little stone hut inside the quarry, the wagtails, or *tinners* as they are called in West Cornwall, would run in and feed at their feet.

On my return, in the spring of 1907, to this place I found a pair of wheatears in possession; they had fought the wagtails and driven them away and made their nest in the same place. The same kindly protection was given to them as to the old favourites, though they never became so tame; and I saw the young safely brought off.

We have seen in a former chapter that the robin is somewhat of a sacred bird, or at all events that the feeling in its favour, superstitious or not, is so general that even in the darkest part of the country the bird when caught in a gin is released and allowed to fly away, to perish of its hurts or drag out a miserable existence in a maimed condition. This feeling is a great protection to the bird, but in many boys the bird-hunting and nest-destroying passion overmasters it, so that I am not greatly surprised when I find boys persecuting robin redbreast.

One very warm morning in early spring, walking uphill from Penzance to Castle-an-Dinas, I came on two boys, aged about ten and eleven respectively, lying on the green turf by the side of the hedge. A nice place to rest and nice company; so I threw myself down by them and started talking, naturally about the birds. They replied reluctantly, exchanging glances and looking very uncomfortable. There were plenty of nests now, I said; I was finding a good many, and I asked them directly how many they knew of with eggs and young birds in them. Seeing that I put it that way they recovered courage, and one, after a brief whispered consultation with the other, said that there was a robin's nest close to my side, and on looking round I spied a fully-fledged young robin standing on a trodden-down little nest on the bank-side. I picked the bird up and was surprised at its docility, for it made no effort to escape, and then, more surprising still, the old bird flew down and perched a yard off, but did not appear at all anxious about the safety of its young. "I wonder," said I, "what has become of the others? There must have been more young robins in this nest—it looks as if it had had three or four to tread it down."

Whereupon one of the boys produced a second robin from his jacket pocket, and when I took it from him the other boy pulled out two more robins from his pockets and handed them to me.

"Now look here," I began in my severest tone, and proceeded to give them a lecture on their unkindness in taking young robins, and did not forget to quote Blake on the subject, for of all birds the robin was the least fitted to be made a prisoner, and so on until I finished.

But the boys showed no sense of guilt or repentance and were no more disturbed at my words than the robins were at being handled, and at length one of them said that they had no intention of taking the birds home.

"What, then, did you have them in your pockets for?" I demanded.

He replied that they put them in their pockets just to keep them out of my sight. They were playing with the birds when I found them, and they had known the nest since it was made, and every day after the young had come out one or both of them had paid them a visit, and they always brought a small supply of caterpillars to feed the robins with.

It was quite true, the tameness of the four young robins sitting on our hands and knees was a proof of it. From time to time while we sat there with them the old birds flew down near us just to take a look round as it seemed and then flew off again, but by-and-by when we put them back on their little platform the parents came and fed them close to our side.

SOME EARLY FLOWERS

BIRDS are perhaps too much to me; at all events, I find that an entire chapter has been written on the coming of spring without a word in it about flowers; it was nearly all taken up with the feathered people. Yet one cannot think of spring without those little touches of moist brilliant colour shining gem-like among the old dead brown leaves and herbage and in all green places. Even here, in a district comparatively flowerless for many months, as I have said, there are flowers to be seen if looked for pretty well all the year round. Just now, before sitting down to write this chapter at the windy bleak Land's End, a very few days be fore Christmas, I went out in the late afternoon, and seeing herb-robert looking very pretty in the shelter of a stone hedge, then some other small flower, and then others, I began idly plucking a spray or two of each, and after crossing three or four fields and home again I found that my little bouquet contained blooms of seventeen different species. If I had gone on a few fields further the number might have been twenty-five or thirty. These little summer and autumn flowers that bloom on till frosts come are all of very common kinds, except, perhaps, the yellow pansy which is confined to the western extremity of the county. There are other flowers proper to the early spring which were a delight to me and which will ever be associated in my mind with the thoughts of Cornwall.

Curiously enough the one which comes first to my mind is a plant universally despised and disliked by the common people and, for all I know to the contrary, by the people who are not common: they speak of it as a "weed" and a "nuisance"; nor is it a spring or summer flower but blooms in mid winter. It is already coming out now, and before the middle of January will be in full bloom. This is the sweet-scented colt's-foot, sometimes called winter heliotrope, on account both of the purple colour and powerful scent of the flower. The books say that it smells of vanilla, also that the plant is an alien, but when introduced they do not say. The *Victorian History of Cornwall* does not mention such a plant. I have looked at the MS. work of John Rolfe (1878) on the plants of West Cornwall, in the Penzance Library, but he does not tell us how long ago it ran wild in this district. It flourishes greatly at Penzance, St. Ives and many of the neighbouring villages, rooting itself in the stone hedges and covering them entirely with a marvellously beautiful garment of round, disc-shaped, flat leaves, of all sizes from that of a crown piece to that of a dessert plate, all of the most vivid green in nature. The flowers, of a dim lilac-purple, are on thick straight stems which spring directly from the roots, and, like sweet violets, they are mostly hidden by the luxuriant leaves. The leaves, which come in winter and spring, last pretty well all the year round, and the roots, the gardeners say, are enormous, and as they push through the crevices and wind themselves about among the stones it is impossible to get rid of the plant.

One of the prettiest scenes I witnessed in West Cornwall is associated with this plant. I saw a girl of about seventeen, small for her age and of a slim figure, come out of a cottage door and walk down to the little garden gate just as I came abreast of it. At the gate was a little foot-bridge over a stream which rushed by with a good deal of noise and foam over the rocks in its bed. The stone hedges and detached masses of rock on both sides of the bridge were covered over with an enormous growth of colt's-foot, the plants flowing over into the stream and even covering some of the big boulder stones in it. That was the setting and the girl was worthy of it, standing there, fresh from the wash-tub, her arms bare to the shoulders, in her thin blue cotton gown, regarding me with lively inquisitive eyes. She had the double attraction of prettiness and singularity. It was a Cornish face, healthy but colourless as in the majority of the women, very broad, high cheek-bones; but it differed in the fineness of the features and in the pointed chin which together with the large eyes gave it that peculiar interesting cat like form seen in some pretty women, and which is so marked in a well-known portrait of Queen Mary at Holyrood. The large eyes were of the greyish blue colour so common in this district, with large pupils and that deepening of colour at the outer edge of the iris which takes the appearance of a black ring. These ringed blue eyes are sometimes seen in other counties, but are most common in the part of Cornwall where I have observed the people. Finally, in strange contrast with the large blue eyes her hair was black, and being unbound the wind was blowing it all about her face and neck.

I stopped to talk to the girl and had plenty of time to get my mental sketch of her. Speaking of the colt's-foot, so abundant at her own door, she told me that she had never heard it named anything but "weed." She also assured me that she hated it, and so did everyone, and she could see nothing to admire in it.

At Penzance a gardener told me he had been fighting this weed all his life and that his father before him had fought with it all his life, so that it must have established itself in that place a very long time ago.

At Madron, the famous and beautiful old village on the heights above Penzance, I saw a curious thing in January 1907. A great part of the extensive churchyard is covered with colt's-foot, and after it had come into bloom the whole of the mass of vivid green leaves was killed by the great frost I have described in Chapter 15, but strange to say the flowers were not hurt. The ground was covered with the upright thick stems, crowned with their pale purple fragrant flowers, and beneath them, dead and brown and flat on the earth, lay the leaves that lately hid them with their multitudinous green discs.

One day, meeting some boys by the side of a hedge overgrown with colt's-foot, I asked them what they called the plant, and was answered by the biggest boy, who knew most, that it was called "rat plant." It was named so, perhaps, because a rat could take shelter in the leaves and run very freely about among them without being seen. Or it may be that the name was bestowed to express a feeling of dislike and contempt— the idea that it was a vegetable rat, something to be warred against, dug up and if possible extirpated. It is a pleasure to me to think we can no more get rid of *Petasites fragrans*, alias "rat-plant," than we can of *Mus decumanus* itself, or *Blatta orientalis*, or any other of the undesirable aliens, plant or animal, which succeed in defying our best efforts to oust them.

Perhaps some of my sober-minded readers, who know the colt's-foot and have not seen its beauty, may smile at my enthusiasm even as I have smiled at my Cornish landlady's story of Billy and his enthusiasm for another species of wild flower. Billy is a youth of about twenty, son of a small farmer in one of the villages I stayed at. This, like most of the villages on this coast, receives its quota of summer visitors who come from distant inland towns, and some of these found accommodation at Billy's parents' farm. They were ladies, and Billy was greatly impressed with their beauty and affability, their dainty dresses, and the nice way in which they passed the time, strolling about, sketching, reading, lying on the turf, and sitting in picturesque attitudes on the rocks. But what perhaps interested him most was the keen pleasure they took in the common natural objects, of the place, especially the wild flowers. They talked to Billy on the subject with the result that he, too, became an admirer of wild flowers, greatly to the amusement of his neighbours.

One day my landlady, going along the village street, saw Billy driving home in the farm trap with what looked like a gigantic yellow buttonhole in his coat. "Why, Billy, whatever have you got there?" she cried when he pulled the horse up to speak to her. "Flowers," said Billy. "I saw them in a cornfield, and I left the horse and went right out into the middle of the field to get them. Ain't they pretty?" And taking the bunch, the stems of which he had thrust into his top pocket, he handed it down for her to admire.

"Goodness me, boy, it's nothing but charlock!" she exclaimed.

"Yes, I know," said Billy. "And they are very pretty; just you look at them—perhaps you never knew how pretty they are." Then he added sententiously, "They are flowers, and all flowers are beautiful."

"Dear, dear!" said she for only reply, handing him back his bouquet.

"When I get home," continued Billy, "I'll put them in water to keep them fresh and set them on the table," and away he drove.

Billy with his charlock flowers reminds me of an incident on a farm in Hampshire where I was staying. The farmer was a hard-headed and very hard-working man absorbed in the great business of keeping his farm like a farm and of making it pay. Tares, turnip-fly, charlock, couch grass and their like—these were his enemies which he hated. And his wife was his worthy helpmate.

One day I brought in a big bunch of poppies, and after, arranging them on their tall stems with some feathery grasses in a vase I put them on the table just laid for the midday meal. The farmer came in fresh from his work, his mind as usual absorbed in his affairs, and first taking up the carving-knife and fork hurriedly said, "For what we are about to receive," and was just going to plunge the fork into the joint when he caught sight of the splendid flowers before him on his own table, audaciously smiling their scarlet smile right at him.

"What are those?" he said, pointing with his knife at the flowers and addressing his wife in no pleasant tones. "What does this mean?"

She cast down her eyes and kept silence.

"I can tell you," I said. "I gathered them myself in one of your fields and put them on the table much against your wife's wish. I can't imagine why she objected. It is one of our finest wild flowers—I call it the Farmer's Glory."

"The Farmer's Glory!—Oh, that's what you call it—well—" and then he suddenly sat down and began carving with tremendous energy and in grim silence.

My pen has run away with me, since I had the images of but two or three wild flowers in my mind to write about in this chapter—flowers of the early spring only—and then the winter heliotrope came up and would not be denied. True, it was of the winter, like Kirke White's "Rosemary"—

> Sweet-scented flower! who art wont to bloom
> On January's fromt severe.
> And o'er the wintry desert drear
> To waft thy sweet perfume—

still, I had to write about it. A flower, like a bird or anything in nature, is little to me unless it "ministers some particular cause of remembrance," which means in my case that either on account of its intrinsic beauty or charm or of its associations it moves my emotions more strongly than others.

The colt's-foot having come first, there are but two others to speak particularly of—a yellow and a blue flower. But the yellow is the furze, so important a flower in this part of England and so much to me, that it must have a chapter to itself, so that in this chapter there will be but one described; but I shall speak of others incidentally and of several things besides.

In my early spring rambles I found that blue flowers were more abundant than all of other colours put together; but this was in the rough places and lanes and by the stone and furze hedges. Here in places almost all the flowers appeared to be blue, from the tall blue columbine to the small ground ivy and the tiniest veronica. Of these I think the most remarkable was the wild hyacinth on account of its habit of growing on the tops of the old stone hedges. The effect is not so charming as when we see them covering the ground under the trees; but it is most singular and beautiful too when the band of blue has the furze bushes covered with yellow blossoms for background.

One April day I had a talk with a native about the blue flowers which were abundant and in great variety at the side of the path. This was on the slope of a hill looking to the sea, about a mile from Mousehole. I saw a girl crossing a grass field, and as she was making for a gate opening on to the path I waited for her and when she came out we went on together for some distance. She had been to take her father his dinner in a field where he was working and was now on her way back to their cottage. Her age was about nineteen or twenty and she was of the most common type found in these parts—short, strongly built, somewhat dumpy; a blonde with grey or bluish-grey eyes, light fluffy hair, and broad, colourless face. There was not a good feature in it, yet it did not strike one as homely, but was pleasant to look at on account of the lively, intelligent and good-natured expression. Finally, she was not flustered or put out in the least degree at being spoken to and joined in her walk by a stranger, but conversed freely with me in that simple natural frank way which seems to me the usual way in Cornwall.

Mr. Ford Madox Hueffer, in his book *The Heart of the Country*, has a good deal to say about the separation of the classes in rural England—the great impassable gulf which exists between gentleman and peasant. As an instance of this he relates that one evening, when walking from a station to the village he was staying at, he overtook a young woman going the same way, and keeping together they conversed quite naturally and pleasantly until they got to the end of the dark lane to where there was a lamp, when it was revealed to the young woman that her companion was not of her own class. "Why," she exclaimed, staring at him in astonishment, "you are a gentleman!" And with that took to her heels and vanished in the dark.

Such an incident would read like a fable in Cornwall—in West Cornwall at all events—for it could not possibly happen there. The caste feeling so common elsewhere hardly exists, and if a gentleman speaks to a young woman in a quiet lane she does not suspect that he has any designs on her nor feel any sense of awe or strangeness to make her silent or awkward. She talks to him as naturally as to one of her own class. It is this common bond between people which one finds a relief and pleasure when going from an English, or an Anglo-Saxon, county to Cornwall and which made it pleasant to me to walk with this homely commonplace peasant girl.

But when I talked to her about the flowers growing in profusion by the hedge-side and along the borders of the path she assured me that she never looked at them and knew nothing about them. Well, yes, she did know three or four wild flowers by their names.

"But surely," I said, "you must know these that are so common—these little blue flowers, for instance, what do you call them?" and I plucked a spray of speedwell. She said they were violets, and when I picked a violet and pointed out the difference in shape and size and colour she agreed that they were a little unlike when you looked at them, "but," she said, "we never look at them and we call all these little blue ones violets." "But," I persisted, "flowers are the most beautiful things on the earth and we all love and admire them and are glad to see them again in spring—surely you must know something more than you say about them—you must have been accustomed to gather them in your childhood." But she would not have it. "We never take notice of wild flowers," she said; "they are no use and we call them all violets—all these blue ones." And she pointed to the hedge-side, where there were violet, forget-me-not, bird's-eye and ground ivy all growing together.

The poor girl did not know much—less than most, perhaps—even less than Billy of the charlock bouquet who had got the one parrot phrase that all flowers are beautiful in his brain; but that which I sought in her and in the pretty, lively Cornish, kitten-like girl already described, and in dozens more, does not come from reading books, nor is it found only in the intelligent. That something lacking in them which you can find by seeking in the more stolid and seemingly duller Anglo-Saxon peasant is of the race.

But enough of adventures in this vain quest of the elusive spirit of romance or poetry. It still remains to speak of the early spring flowers, and of the blue one, which was no common and universal flower like those I have just mentioned, but one I had never seen growing wild until I came to Cornwall. This was the vernal squill, a small blue lily-shaped flower of a delicate, very beautiful blue, hardly deeper than that of the hairbell, growing in clusters of three or four on a polished stalk an inch or two or three in height. The stem varies in length according to the depth of the grass or herbage or dwarf heath among which it grows, as the flower likes to keep itself on a level with the surface of the grass, or nestling in it, like a stone in its setting. In April I first found it, a flower or two here and there, in small depressions and on sunny slopes sheltered from the blast by the huge rocks of the headlands: it was one of the few first early flowers which produce that most fairy-like beautifying effect on these castled promontories, blossoming at the feet of and among the rugged masses of granite overgrown with coarse grey lichen.

By-and-by I was delighted to find that these few scattered blooms were but the first corners of an innumerable multitude, for day by day and week by week the number of them increased, first keeping to the sunniest and most sheltered places, then spreading until they were everywhere along the coast. But always within its own curiously narrow limit, blooming close to the cliff, in some places right to the very brink, but usually some yards back from it, distributed over the ground to a breadth of a dozen or fifteen yards, thus forming a band. Where the soil is favourable and the flowers abundant the band is very conspicuous, and in places where the land slopes to the cliff it broadens and occupies the ground to a breadth of fifty to a hundred yards or even more, then narrows again and pursues its way, following the numberless indentations of the coast line, climbing up and down the steep slopes and sides of gullies and fading and almost vanishing on the barren heath on the highest cliffs.

Now when I first saw the vernal squill, when it had been nothing in my mind but a little blue flower with a pretty book name, it captivated me with its delicate loveliness—its little drop of cerulean colour in a stony desolate place—and with its delightful perfume, but it certainly did not affect me greatly as I have been affected time and again by other flowers, first seen in the greatest profusion and in their best aspect. The commonest of all flowers, the buttercup, is one of these, as I first beheld it covering whole meadows with its pure delicately brilliant yellow. I remember at the end of the African War coming up one day in April from Southampton in a train full of soldiers just back from the veldt, and when a meadow bright with buttercups came in sight the men in my compartment all jumped up and shouted with joy. That sight made them realise as no other could have done, that they were at home once more in England. The wild hyacinth is another flower which took a distinguished place in my mind from the first moment of its coming before my sight, a sea of misty blue beneath the woodland trees in their tender early spring foliage. Another is the gorse from the day I looked on a wide common aflame with its bloom; still another the briar rose, first beheld in the greatest luxuriance and abundance on a vast unkept hedge in Southern England. Then, too, the fritillary on the occasion of my first finding it growing wild in a water-meadow and standing, as in a field of corn, knee-deep amidst the tens and hundreds of thousands of crowded slender stems with their nodding pendulous tulips so strangely chequered with darkest purple and luminous pink. But over all the revelations of the glory of flowers I have experienced in this land I hold my first sight of heather in bloom on the Scottish moors in August shortly after coming to this country. I remember how I went out and walked many miles over the moors, lured ever on by the sight of that novel loveliness until I was lost in a place where no house was visible, and how at intervals when the sun broke through the clouds and shone on some distant hill or slope from which the grey mist had just lifted, revealing the purple colour beneath, it appeared like a vision of the Delectable Mountains.

From the flowers which are greatest only because of their numbers, seeing that, comparing flower with flower, they are equalled and surpassed in lustre by very many other species, it may appear a far descent to my little inconspicuous lily by the sea. For what was there beyond the mere fact of its rarity to make it seem more than many others—than herb-robert in the hedge, for instance, or any small delicate red geranium or brighter lychnis; or, to come to its own colour, veronica with its "darling blue," and, lovelier still, water forget-me-not, with a yellow pupil to its turquoise iris; or the minute bird-shaped blue milkwort, and gentian and bluebell and hairbell and borage and periwinkle and blue geranium, and that delicate rarity the blue pimpernel, and the still rarer and more beautiful blue anemone? Nevertheless, after many days with this unimportant little flower, one among many, from its earliest appearance, when it blossomed sparingly at the foot of the rock, to the time when it had increased and spread to right and left and formed that blue-sprinkled band or path by which I walked daily by the sea, often sitting or lying on the turf the better to inhale its delicious perfume, it came to be more to me than all those unimportant ones which I have named, with many others equally beautiful, and was at last regarded as among the best in the land. For it had entered into my soul, and was among flowers an equal of the briar rose and honeysuckle in the English hedges and of the pale and van-coloured Cornish heath as I saw it in August in lonely places among the Goonhilly Downs in the Lizard district, and, like that heath, it had become for ever associated in my mind with the thought of Cornwall.

Its charm was due both to its sky-colour and perfume and its curious habit of growing just so far and no further from the edge of the cliff; so that when I walked by the sea I had that blue-flecked path constantly before me. One day I made the remark mentally that it appeared as if the sky itself, the genius or blue lady of the sky, had come down to walk by the sea and had left that sky-colour on the turf where she had trailed her robe, and this shade or quality of the hue set me thinking of a chapter I once wrote on the "Secret of the Charm of Flowers" (*Birds and Man*, pp. 111–13), in which the peculiar pleasure which certain flowers produce in us was traced to their human colouring—in other words, the *expression* was due to human associations. Some of my friends would not accept this view, and although I still believe it the right one I became convinced in the course of the argument of a grave omission in my account of the blue flower—that it was unconsciously associated with the blue eye in man and received its distinctive expression from this cause alone. One of my correspondents, anxious to prove me wrong, quoted an idea expressed by someone that flowers are beautiful and precious to us because, apart from their intrinsic charm of colour, fragrance and form, they are absolutely unrelated to our human life with its passions, sorrows and tragedies; and, finally, he said of the blue flower, that if it had any associations at all they were not human; the suggestion was of the blue sky, the open air, of fair weather. It was so in his own case—"I can feel the different blues of skies and air and distances in flower blue."

Undoubtedly he was right as to the fair-weather suggestion in the blue flower—I could not look at the vernal squill without feeling convinced of it. Then, oddly enough, another correspondent who was also among my opponents kindly sent me this striking passage from an old writer, Sir John Ferne, on azure in blazonry:

> Which blew colour representeth the Aire amongst the elements, that of all the rest is the greatest favourer of life, as the only nurse and maintainer of spirits in any living creature. The colour blew is commonly taken from the clear skye which appeareth so often as the tempests be overblowne, and notes prosperous successe and good fortune to the wearer in all his affayres.

My view now is that the human association is a chief factor in the expression of blue flowers in some species, such as pansy, violet, speedwell and various others, which bloom sparsely and are seen distinctly as single flowers and not as mere splashes of colour; and that with blue flowers seen in masses, as in the case of the wild hyacinth and sometimes the viper's bugloss, the association is more with the clear blue sky. But doubtless both elements are present in all cases, that is to say with our race; among dark-eyed people the expression of the blue flower would have the fair-weather association alone.

THE FURZE IN ITS GLORY

I THINK that of all plants indigenous in this island the furze delights me the most. This says a good deal for a man who takes as much pleasure as anyone in green and growing things; in all of them, from the elm of greatest girth at Windsor or Badminton, or the noblest pine at Eversley, or the most aged oak at Aldermaston, down to the little ivy-leafed toad-flax growing on the wall. They move me, each in its way, according to its character, to admiration, love and reverence. No sooner do I begin to speak or even to think of them than they, or their images, are seen springing up as by a miracle round me, until I seem to be in a vast open forest where all beautiful things flourish exceedingly and each in turn claims my attention. Merely to name them, with just a word or two added to characterise the special feeling produced in each case, would fill a page or more; and the end of it all would be that the words used at the beginning would have to be said again—I think the furze is the one which pleases me best.

Now here is something which has been a puzzle to me and a cause of regret, or a sense of something missed—the fact that, excepting a word or two or a line about it in the poets, the furze is hardly to be found in literature. Think of the oak in this connection; think of the elm, the yew, the ash, the rowan, the holly, hawthorn, blackthorn, bramble, briar, bulrush and flowering rush and heather, with many, many more trees, bushes and herbs, down even to the little pimpernel, the daisy, the forget-me-not and the lesser celandine. But who, beyond a line or two, has ever in verse or prose said anything in praise of the furze?

One day, in conversation with Sir William Thiselton-Dyer, the late Director of Kew Gardens, who knows a great deal more of books about plants than I do, I mentioned this fact to him, and, after taking thought, he said, "It is true, there isn't much to find, but let me recommend you to read Evelyn."

It happened that I knew Evelyn and admired him for his noble diction: one really wonders how a man who looked at plants with his hard, utilitarian eyes, considering them solely for their uses, could write as he did. It is true that he saw some beauty in the holly, his favourite, but in little else. He mentions the furze as a "vegetable trifle," and even goes so far as to give it a few favourable words, but without anything about its appearance, for that did not touch him. It is not a wholly useless plant, says Evelyn; it is good for faggots, also it affords covert for wild fowl, and the tops (bruised) may be recommended for a sickly horse. "It will thoroughly recover and plump him."

I have often watched the semi-wild ponies of the New Forest browsing quite freely on the blossomed tops, which they bruised for themselves with their own molars; and now I know that the furze is also "good for faggots." I have described how, while staying at a small moorland farm during the winter, we had furze for fuel, and how the dried bushes made a glorious heat and illumination in the open wide fireplace of the old dark kitchen and living-room. A couple of months later when the plant was in full blossom—acres and miles and leagues of it—I could do no less than sing my poor little prose song of praise and gratitude. To me it is never "unprofitably gay," nor, when I handle it, does it wound my hardened fingers, causing me to recoil and cry out with the sensitive poet of the *Task* that it repels us with its treacherous spines as much as it attracts with its yellow bloom.

The beauty of the furze in flower—that special beauty and charm in which it excels all other plants—is an effect of contrast, and is a beauty only seen in the entire plant, over which the bloom is distributed. We see that in shape and size, and almost in colour, the blossom nearly resembles that of the broom, but the effect is far more beautiful on account of the character of the plant—the exceeding roughness of its spiny surface, the rude shapes it takes and its darkness, over which the winged flame-coloured blossoms are profusely sprinkled. And when we see many contiguous bushes they do not lose their various individual forms, nor do the blossoms, how ever abundant, unite, as is the case with the broom, into very large masses of brilliant colour.

I like to come upon a furze-patch growing on a slope, to sit below it and look up over its surface, thrown into more or less rounded forms, broken and roughened into sprays at the top, as of a sea churned by winds and cross-currents to lumpy waves, all splashed and crowned as it were with flame-coloured froth. With a clear blue sky beyond I do not know in all nature a spectacle to excel it in beauty. It is beautiful, perhaps above all things, just because the blossoming furze is not the "sheet of gold" it is often described, but gold of a flame-like brilliance sprinkled on a ground of darkest, harshest green. Sheets of brilliant colour are not always beautiful. I have looked on leagues of forest of *Erythrina cristagalli* covering a wet level marsh when the leafless trees were clothed in their blood-red blossoms and have not admired the spectacle. Again, I have ridden through immense fields of viper's bugloss, growing as high as the horse's breast and so dense that he could hardly force his way through it, and the sheet of vivid blue in a dazzling sunlight affected me very disagreeably. It is the same with cultivated fields of daffodils, tulips and other flowers, grown to supply the market; the sight pleases best at a distance of a mile or half a mile; and so in the case of a sheet of wild hyacinths, it delights the eye because it is seen under trees with a cloud of green foliage above to soften and bring the vivid hue into harmony with the general colouring.

Now in the furze, or the dark green prickly sprays, the colour and roughness of which are never wholly covered and extinguished by the blossoms, there is an appearance which has probably never been described and perhaps not observed. The plant, we see, changes its colour somewhat with the seasons. It is darkest in winter, when, seen at a distance on the pale green or grey-green chalk downs, it looks almost black. Again, in summer when the rusty appearance which follows the flowering time is put off, the new terminal sprays have a blue-green or glaucous hue like the pine and juniper. But the most interesting change, which contributes to the beauty of the furze at its best, is in the spring, when the spines are tipped with straw-yellow and minute lines of the same colour appear along the spines and finer stems, and the effect of these innumerable specks and lines which catch the light is to give a bronzed appearance to the dark mass. It is curious that that change of colour does not always take place; in many places you find the plants keep the uniform deep green of winter through the blossoming season; but the bronzed aspect is the loveliest, and makes the most perfect setting for the bloom.

There are few things in nature that more delight the eye than a wild common or other incult place overgrown with bramble mixed with furze in flower and bracken in its vivid green, and scattered groups or thickets of hawthorn and blackthorn, with tangles and trails of ivy, bryony, traveller's joy and honeysuckle. Yet the loveliness of our plant in such surroundings is to my mind exceeded by the furze when it possesses the entire ground and you have its splendour in fullest measure. Then, too, you can best enjoy its fragrance. This has a peculiar richness, and has been compared with pineapple and cocoa-nut; I should say cocoanut and honey, and we might even liken it to apple-tart with clove for scent and flavour. Anyway, there is something fruity and appetising in the smell; but this is not all, since along with that which appeals to the lower sense there is a more subtle quality, ethereal and soul-penetrating, like the perfume of the mignonette, the scented orchis, violet, bog asphodel, narcissus and vernal squill. It may be said that flower-scents are of two sorts: those which, like fruits, suggest flavours, and those which are wholly unassociated with taste, and are of all odours the most emotional because of their power of recalling past scenes and events. In the perfume of the furze both qualities, the sensuous and the spiritual, are combined: doubtless it was the higher quality which Swinburne had in his mind when he sang:

The whin was frankincense and flame.

But we regard vision as the higher or more intellectual sense, and seeing is best; and it was the sight of blossoming furze which caused Linn on his first visit to England, when he was taken to see it at Putney Heath, to fall on his knees and thank God for creating so beautiful a plant.

I bring in this old story so that the cynical reader may not be cheated of his smile. He it is who said, and I believe he has had even the courage to print it, that there was nothing spontaneous in the act of the great Swedish naturalist, that he had rehearsed it beforehand, and doubtless dropped upon his knees several times in front of a pier-glass in his bedroom that very morning to make himself perfect in the action before being driven to Putney.

Linnæus is good enough for me, and for the majority of us I imagine, but what shall we say of the mockers, the spiritual harpies who come unbidden to our sacred feasts to touch and handle everything, and to defile and make hateful whatsoever they touch? Alas, we cannot escape and cannot silence them, and may only say that we com passionate them; since, however great they may be in the world, and though intellectually they may be but little lower than the gods, yet do they miss all that is sweetest and most precious in life. And further, we can only hope that when they have finished their little mocking day, that which they now are may be refashioned by wonderful Nature into some better thing—a dark, prickly bush, let us say, with blossoms that are frankincense and flame.

Let this same fragrance sweeten our imaginations; or, better still, let us forget that such beings exist in the world—with atrophied hearts—and see what the furze looks like in this Land's End district where it most abounds and the earth is clothed with it. In some places where the moorland has been reclaimed and parcelled out into grass fields the furze flourishes on the stone hedges: the effect is here singular as well as magnificent, when, standing on a high stone wall, you survey the surrounding country with innumerable furze-clothed hedges dividing the green fields around you in every direction, and appearing like stupendous ropes of shining golden bloom. Hedge beyond hedge they stretch away for miles to grey distant hills and the pale blue sky beyond. On some hedges the plant grows evenly, as if it had been cultivated and trimmed, forming a smooth rope of bloom and black prickles. In other and indeed most instances, the rounded big luxuriant bushes occur at intervals, like huge bosses, on the rope.

Walking by one of these hedges in a very strong sunlight about mid-May when the bloom is in its greatest perfection, the sight is actually dazzling and hurts by the intense luminous colour. It is an unusual experience, but after a mile or so one almost unconsciously averts or veils the eye in passing one of these splendid bushes on which, the blossoms are too closely crowded.

Perhaps the best aspect of the plant is that of the rough unreclaimed places where the high land slopes down to the cliff and the furze grows luxuriantly along the edges and slopes of the deep clefts or little ravine-like valleys, the beds of crystal noisy little water-courses, peopled with troutlets no bigger than minnows. Here the rude, untamable plant has its wildest and most striking appearance, now in the form of a huge mound where several bushes are closely interwoven, and now growing separately like ancient dwarf trees, mixed with brown heath and grey masses of granite. Here, too, you may come upon a clump of dwarf blackthorn bushes thickly covered with their luminous crystalline white little roses, never looking so wonderful in their immaculate whiteness as when thus seen contrasted with the rough black and flame-colour of the furze.

Better still, you can here see the yellow and orange flame of the furze against the blue of the sea—a marvellously beautiful effect. I was reminded of a similar effect observed in a furzy place among the South Wiltshire downs a year before. It was one of those days when there are big dark masses of cloud in a clear sky and when the cloud shadows falling on distant woods and hills give them a deep indigo blue. The furze was in full bloom and had a new and strange glory in my eyes when seen against this deep blue of the distant landscape.

Yellow and blue—yellow and blue! A lady on the other side of the globe wrote complaining that these two colours in association had got on her nerves on account of something I had said in some book. That was the fault of the writing. In nature they never get on our nerves: they surprise us, because the sight is not an everyday one, and in some cases where they occupy a large field they intoxicate the mind with their unparalleled loveliness. It has ever been a delight to me just before harvest time to walk in fine weather near the sea just to look at the red gold of the ripe corn against the blue water. We get a similar effect from these two complementary colours at sunset when the clouds are flushed yellow and orange in blue sky. Also in the beech woods in October the sight of the great trees in their magnificent red–gold foliage would not impress us so deeply but for the blue sky seen through and above the wood.

PILGRIMS AT THE LAND'S END

I RECALL now that I did not come to Cornwall to write a book about it, or any part of it. But like many others I had to see the Land's End; and it was winter, when the Wiltshire Downs, where it was my desire to be, are bleak, and I had a cold to get rid of, so I came to the "rocky land of strangers," to look once in my life on the famous headland and return with the wheatear and stone curlew to the lonely green hills. Being here I put down some impressions of gulls and fishing-boats at St. Ives for a weekly journal; other impressions followed, and because the place held me month after month, and the old habit of taking notes, or stick-gathering, even when the sticks are of no more use than the vast store of stolen objects which my friend's pet white rat, who has the run of a big house, is accustomed to accumulate, the material grew on my hands, until in the end I determined to put the best of it in a volume. In that way the book and every chapter grew. One chapter, headed "Bolerium," contained my impressions of the famous headland itself, and having written it I imagined there would be no more for me to say on that subject. Nevertheless, I continued to haunt the spot; familiarity had not lessened its fascination, and there, by chance, one day in spring, I witnessed a scene which suggested, or perhaps I should say compelled me to write, this additional chapter as a conclusion to the book.

There were days at the headland when I observed a goodish number of elderly men among the pilgrims, some very old, and this at first surprised me, but by-and-by it began to seem only natural. I was particularly impressed one day at noon in early spring in clear but cold weather with a biting north east wind, when I found six or seven aged men sitting about on the rocks that lie scattered over the green slope behind the famous promontory. They were too old or too feeble to venture down on the rough headland: their companions had strayed away, some to the fishing cove, others along the higher cliffs and left them there to rest. They were in great-coats with scarves and comforters round their necks, and hats or caps drawn well down; and they sat mostly in dejected attitudes, bending forward, their hands resting on the handles of their sticks, some with their chins on their hands, but all gazed in one direction over the cold grey sea. Strangers to each other, unlike in life and character, coming from widely separated places, some probably from countries beyond the ocean, yet all here, silently gazing in one direction beyond that rocky foreland, with the same look of infinite weariness on their grey faces and in their dim sad eyes, as if one thought and feeling and motive had drawn them to this spot. Can it be that the sentiment or fancy which is sown in our minds in childhood and lies asleep and forgotten in us through most of our years, revives and acquires towards the end a new and strange significance when we have entered upon our second childhood? The period, I mean, when we recover our ancient mental possessions—the heirlooms which cannot be alienated or lost, which have descended to us from our remotest progenitors through centuries and thousands of years. These old men cannot see the objects which appear to younger eyes—the distant passing ships, and the land— that dim, broken line, as of a low cloud on the horizon, of the islands: their sight is altered from what it was, yet is, perhaps, now able to discern things invisible to us—other islands, uncharted, not the Cassiterides. What are they, these other islands, and what do we know of them? Nothing at all; indeed, nothing can be known to the generality; only these life-weary ancients, sitting on rocks and gazing at vacancy, might enlighten us if they would. Undoubtedly there are differences of sight among them which would make their descriptions vary, but they would probably all agree in affirming that the scene before them has no resemblance to the earlier vision. This grey-faced very old man with his chin on his hands, who looks as if he had not smiled these many years, would perhaps smile now if he were to recall that former vision, which came by teaching and served well enough during his hot youth and strenuous middle age. He does not see before him a beautiful blessed land bright with fadeless flowers, nor a great multitude of people in shining garments and garlands who will come down to the shore to welcome him with sounds of shouting and singing and playing on instruments of divers forms, and who will lead him in triumph to the gardens of everlasting delight and to mansions of crystal with emerald and amethyst colonnades and opal domes and turrets and pinnacles. Those glories and populous realms of joy have quite vanished: he sees now only what his heart desires—a silent land of rest. No person will greet him there; he will land and go up alone into that empty and solitary place, a still grey wilderness extending inland and upward hundreds of leagues, an immeasurable distance, into infinity, and rising to mountain ridges compared with which the Himalayas are but mole-hills. The sky in that still land is always pale grey-blue in colour, and the earth, too, is grey like the rocks, and the trees have a grey-green foliage—trees more ancient in appearance than the worn granite hills, with gnarled and buttressed trunks like vast towers and immense horizontal branches, casting a slight shade over many acres of ground. Onwards and upwards, with eyes downcast, he will slowly take his devious way to the interior, feeling the earth with his staff, in search of a suitable last resting-place. And when he has travelled many, many leagues and has found it—a spot not too sunny nor too deeply shaded, where the old fallen dead leaves and dry moss have formed a thick soft couch to recline on and a grey exposed root winding over the earth offers a rest to his back—there at length he will settle himself. There he will remain motionless and contented for ever in that remote desert land which is no sound of singing bird nor of running water nor of rain or wind in the grey ancient trees: waking and sleeping he will rest there, dreaming little and thinking less, while year by year and age by age the memory of the world of passion and striving of which he was so unutterably tired grows fainter and fainter in his mind. And he will have neither joy nor sorrow, nor love nor hate, nor wish to know them any more; and when he remembers his fellow-men it will comfort him to think that his peace will never be broken by the sight of human face or the sound of human speech, since never by any chance will any wanderer from the world discover him in that illimitable wilderness.

This may not have been the precise vision of that old man, sitting on a rock with chin resting on his hands; it is merely my interpretation of his appearance and expression at that spot—his grey weary face, his dejected attitude, his immobility; his and that of the five or six others—those grey old men who, by a strange chance, had all come to the place one day at the same hour, and had been left to their own melancholy thoughts by their younger, more active companions. It was mere chance, but the sight profoundly impressed me and gave me a more vivid idea than I had hitherto had of the fascination this last rocky headland has for our minds.

Then, when the strange spectacle of those aged men on that bleak day, seated, each on his rock, twenty or thirty yards apart, absorbed in his own mournful thoughts and gazing out fixedly on the troubled sea, was still fresh, other incidents came to keep the subject uppermost in my mind and to compel me to return to it and to make in conclusion a practical suggestion.

One of the "incidents" mentioned was the perusal of a book on Cornwall which I picked up in Penzance for the sake of the excellent illustrations rather than to read it. I had already read or glanced through forty or fifty or, it may be, a hundred books on Cornwall with little pleasure or profit and did not want to read any more. It was *An Unsentimental Journey through Cornwall*, by the author of *John Halifax, Gentleman*, a lady who could not be unsentimental if she tried ever so hard.

The book is dated 1884, but a few years before the author's death, when she was a feeble old lady whose long life-work of producing novels was over, and her time in Cornwall was limited to seventeen September days. We are concerned only with her visit to the Land's End, and I quote here a portion of her account of it:

It would be hard if, after journeying thus far and looking forward to it so many years, the day on which we went to the Land's End should turn out a wet day! . . . We wondered for the last time, as we had wondered for half a century, what the Land's End would be like. . . .

At first our thought had been, What in the world shall we do here for two mortal hours? Now we wished we had two whole days. A sunset, a sunrise, a starlit night, what would they have been in this grand lonely place—almost as lonely as a ship at sea!

The bright day was darkening, and a soft greyness began to creep over land and sea. No, not soft, that is the very last adjective applicable to the Land's End. Even on that calm day there was a fresh wind—there must be always a wind—and the air felt sharper and more salt than any sea-air I ever knew, stimulating too, so that our nerves were strung to the highest pitch of excitement. We felt able to do anything without fear and without fatigue. . . . Still, though a narrow and giddy path, there was a path, and the exploit, though a little risky, was not foolhardy. We should have been bitterly sorry not to have done it—not to have stood for one grand ten minutes where in all our lives we may never stand again, at the furthest point where footing is possible, gazing out on that magnificent circle of sea which sweeps over the submerged land of Lyonesse, far, far away into the wide Atlantic.

Half a mile from Marazion the rain ceased, and a light like that of a rising moon began to break through the clouds. What a night it might be, or might have been, could we have stayed at the Land's End!

That ghastly "might have been"! It is in great things as in small, the worry, the torment, the paralysing burden of life. Away with it! We have done our best to be happy and we have been happy. We have seen the Land's End.

Her cheerfulness makes one's eyes moisten—that one day at the Land's End, when her life's work was over, when in spite of her years and weak nerves she ventured painfully down and out among those rough crags, assisted by her guide and companion, for one grand ten minutes on the outermost rock—the fulfilment of a dream of fifty years!

She was a very gentle, tender-hearted woman, as sweet and lovable a soul as ever dwelt on earth, but her mind was only an average one, essentially mediocre; in her numerous works she never rose above the commonplace. There are thousands of women all over the country who could produce as many and as good books as hers if they were industrious enough and thought it worth their while to take up novel-writing as a profession. She wrote for the million and is understood by them, and I take it that in her dream and sentiment about the Land's she represents her public—the mass of the educated women in England—just as she represents their feeling about love and the domestic virtues and life generally in her *John Halifax, Mistress and Maid, A Life for a Life* and scores of other works.

But books, however eloquent and heart-searching they may be, cannot produce an effect comparable to that of seeing and hearing—to the sight and sound of emotion in men's faces and voices and in their words. The passage I have quoted, and all the other passages on the subject in the other books I had read, gave me no such vivid idea of the strength of the sentiment we are considering as did the other incident I wish to relate when, on May 24, at Penzance station, I witnessed the arrival, in four trains, of about twelve hundred trippers from some of the cotton-spinning centres forty or fifty miles north of Manchester. The first train steamed into the station, where a crowd had to see the horde of strange people from the north, at 10.45; the last of the four arrived a little before 12 at noon. The return journey would begin at 6.30 on the same day: the entire distance to and from Penzance was considerably over eight hundred miles; the time it took, twenty-six to twenty-eight hours, and the time the travellers had at their disposal at their destination was about seven hours. I was amazed that twelve hundred men had been found to undertake such a journey just to see Penzance—one of the least interesting towns in the kingdom; but when I mixed with and talked with them on their arrival, they assured me they had not come for such an object and would be content to go back without seeing Penzance. Nor did they come for the sake of anything in fine scenery which Cornwall could show them; North Wales with its bold sea-coast and magnificent mountain scenery was easily accessible to them. What they came to see was the Land's End.

The Cornishmen who were present could not understand this. I talked with one poor fellow, who sat down on a bench looking very pale, saying that after thirteen hours in the train without a wink of sleep he felt very tired; but he was greatly disappointed at not having got a seat in the first lot of conveyances which were driving off loaded with his fellow-travellers to the Land's End, and feared that he might miss seeing it after all. Among those who had gathered round to hear what was said were two old Penzance men and they laughed heartily. "Why," said one, "I've been here within ten miles of the Land's End all my life and have never seen it." "I can say as much, and more," said the other; "I've never seen it and never want to see it." "Perhaps," I remarked, "if you had been born five hundred or five thousand miles away you would have felt differently about it." The poor pale Lancastrian looked pleased. "That's true!" he exclaimed. "I've always wanted to see the Land's End, and it's the same with all of us: we've come to see it and for nothing else."

It was the literal truth, as I found by hanging about and talking with these men from the north all that day, watching them going and returning. But the motor buses, char-à-bancs and other vehicles were not enough to take them all, and when it came to three o'clock and half-past three, and there was but time left to go with all speed, look for a few brief minutes at the rocks, and hasten back in time for the last train, the poor fellows began offering five shillings per man to be driven there and back, and then at the last some offered ten shillings. But it was too late and they could not be taken!

Is this sentiment, which is not confined to our island country but survives in the transplanted race in other regions of the globe, this feeling which the matter-of-fact Cornishman laughs at and which may make many of us smile when we meet with it in a printed book, but is in us all the same and a part of our life—is this sentiment of any value and worth cherishing? I take it that it is, since if we were stripped of sentiment, illusion and such traditions, romance and dreams as we inherit or which gather about and remain with us to the end of our days, we should be beggared indeed. Well, let it be so, it may be said in reply; 'tis in you and in many of us, and some have it not, and that's all there is to be said about it—why then speak of cherishing? For the following reason in this particular case: the sentiment relates to a locality, a spot of land with peculiar features and character, a rocky headland with the boundless ocean in front and the desolate wind-swept moor behind. These features, an image of which is carried in our minds from childhood, are bound up with and are part and parcel of the feeling, so that to make any change in such a spot, to blow up the headland, for instance, as anyone could do with a few shillings' worth of dynamite, or to alter and deface the surface of the adjacent land and build big houses and other ugly structures on it, would be felt by every pilgrim as an indignity, a hateful vandalism. We have seen in the case of Hindhead and of many other places which powerfully attract us, what the greed and philistinism of man will do to destroy an ancient charm. A man may do what he likes with his own— a frightful liberty when we remember how God's footstool has been parcelled out among private persons, and what brutish men, or men without the sense of beauty, have done and may do to spoil it. I suppose that if Sir Edmund Antrobus thought proper he could run up a red-brick hotel or sanatorium high as Hankey's Mansions at Stonehenge: but not Stonehenge, nor Mona, nor Senlac, nor that hoary fane where Britain buries her great dead, nor any castle or cathedral, or tower or river or mountain or plain in all the land draws us so powerfully as this naked moor and rude foreland with its ancient dim memories and associations. And we now see what is being done with it—how plots of land for building purposes are being sold right and left, and the place in every way vulgarised and degraded.

Undoubtedly there are men so devoid of sentiment and imagination that they would not hesitate to stamp out the last beautiful thing on earth, if its beauty, or some sentiment connected with it which made it seem beautiful, is the only reason or the only excuse that can be given for its existence. But all are not of this character, and to those who have something besides Cornish tin and copper in their souls, who are not wholly devoted to their own and, incidentally, to their county's, material prosperity, I would appeal to rescue from degradation and to preserve unspoilt for all time this precious spot to which pilgrims resort from all the land.

It is not necessary, I hope, to describe the Land's End as the county's best "asset" or as the "goose that lays the golden eggs," or by some such abominable phrase, which is yet well understood by all since it appeals to the baser nature in every man—to his greed and his cunning; still, it might be well to remind even those who are wholly concerned with material things that the sentiment they make light of probably exists in some degree in a majority of the inhabitants of this country—be it remembered, is mainly Anglo-Saxon, a sentimental race, to use the word in its better sense—and that it is the desire of most persons to see the Land's End; also that probably nine of every ten visitors to Cornwall think of that headland as their objective point.

To save this spot it would undoubtedly have to be taken from private ownership; and, given the desire, there would be small difficulty in obtaining an Act of Parliament for the compulsory sale of a strip of the sea-front with, let us say, a couple of thousand acres of the adjoining moor. The buildings which now deform the place, the unneeded hotels, with stables, shanties, zinc bungalows sprawling over the cliff, and the ugly big and little houses could be cleared away, leaving only the ancient village of St. Sennen, the old farm-houses, the coastguard and Trinity House stations, and the old fishing hamlet under the cliff.

If a Cornish Society formed for the purpose, and working with the County Council, could not do this without outside help, the money needed could no doubt be easily raised by public subscription. We know that very large sums are frequently given by the public for similar purposes, also for various other purposes which appeal to comparatively very few, as, for example, when the sum of forty-five thousand pounds was recently given by private subscribers to purchase the Rokeby "Venus" for the National Gallery. Yet for every single subscriber to that fund, and, I may say, for every person in England who regards that canvas as a valuable acquisition, there are probably thousands who would gladly see the Land's End made a national possession, and who would willingly subscribe for such an object.

THE END

INDEX

Adder 10, 32, 64, 70, 125, 157,
    158, 161

Badger 29, 80, 150, 151
Bibliotheca Cornubiensis 115
Blackbird 61, 130
Blackthorn 62, 141, 175, 177, 179
Borde, Andrew 69
Borlase, William 115, 153
Bracken 26, 32, 35, 36, 65, 126,
    127, 128, 136, 157, 161
Brett, marine artist 106
Browning, Dramatic Idylls 55
Burgomaster, glaucus gull 21
Bush-beating 130
Buttercup 159, 172

Calderon, Life's a Dream 46
Campbell, Rev. R. J. 82
Cape Cornwall 33, 38
Carew. Richard 26, 85, 87, 115
Carew, Thomas 115
Carter, R. H. 150
Cassiterides (Scilly Islands) 182
Castle-an-Dinas 163
Chaffinch 148, 149
Chiffchaff 161
Collins, Wilkie 39
Columbine, wild 169
Cornwall's Connemara 5, 25, 98,
    99, 125
Corn bunting 10, 65, 161
Courtney, Lord 115, 119
Cow 27, 60

Curlew 151, 181

Darwin, Charles 55
Davy, Sir Humphry 40
Daw 14, 15, 16, 33, 37, 46, 59, 61,
    125, 136, 141, 144
The Dawn in Britain 68
Dewar, G. A. B. 128
Dog 21, 27, 28, 74, 136, 138
Dogfish 21, 68
Donkey 60, 92, 114, 118
Dunnock 161, 162

Ebblethwaite, Mr 133, 134
Evelyn, John 175, 176

Farmers, Cornish 26
Ferne, Sir John 174
Fieldfare 33, 61, 129, 135
Fishermen 7, 11, 22, 54, 56, 57,
    70, 95, 106, 121, 129, 133,
    134, 156
Fishing-boats 7, 181
Fowl 27
Fox 27, 37, 64, 80, 138, 139, 140,
    150
Fritillary 172
Frog 161
Fuller, Thomas 9
Furze 25, 26, 27, 32, 34, 35, 36,
    38, 48, 60, 62, 63, 64, 70,
    74, 112, 126, 127, 128, 129,
    136, 138, 141, 142, 157,
    161, 162, 169, 175, 176,
    177, 178, 179

Gannet 7, 46, 49, 50, 51, 53, 54,
        55, 56, 57, 58
Gilpin, William 25, 119
Godrevy Lighthouse 56, 151
Goldfinch 61
Goonhilly Downs 173
Great northern diver 54, 154
Guillemot 151, 152
Guize-dancing 109
Gull 19, 20, 21, 23, 47, 53, 54, 55,
        56, 57, 112, 113, 114, 150,
        151, 152, 159, 160
Gurnard's Head 38, 48, 53, 158

Hake, Gordon 33
Hawker of Morwenstow 115
Hayle estuary 152
Headlands 37, 38, 45, 47, 126,
        160, 171
Heather 60, 126, 140, 157, 172,
        175
Hedges 28, 32, 33, 34, 35, 36, 43,
        60, 136, 137, 142, 144, 162,
        166, 169, 173, 179
Hook, J. C. 118
Hueffer, Ford Madox 170
Humour, Cornish 97, 98
Hunt, Robert, *Popular Romances of
        the West of England* 120
Hyacinth 169, 172, 174

Ivy 14, 31, 35, 36, 62, 169, 171,
        175, 177

James, Prof. William 82

Kestrel 52, 154

Land's End 1, 3, 5, 7, 8, 9, 10, 25,
        37, 38, 39, 40, 41, 45, 48,
        54, 57, 64, 74, 80, 106, 129,
        135, 150, 165, 178, 181,
        184, 185, 186, 187, 188
Launce 56
Lelant 13, 137, 146
Lizard lights 41
Logan Stone 38
Longships 41

Madron 167
Magpie 26, 32, 62, 63
Marazion 25, 79, 184
Market Jew Street 76, 80
Methodism 40, 42, 71, 84, 85,
        121, 122, 123
Montgomery, James, *Pelican Island*
        46
Moore, Sturge, poem on *Wings*
        46
Mount's Bay 25, 37, 64, 79, 135
Mousehole 25, 79, 169

Newlyn 25, 79
Norden on Cornish speech 69,
        91

Osprey 154

Pearce, J. H., *Cornish Drolls* 41
Penzance 5, 7, 14, 25, 38, 39, 76,
        79, 80, 81, 82, 83, 84, 106,
        107, 119, 120, 163, 166,
        167, 184, 185, 186
Phillack 137, 146
Pig 27, 33, 74
Pipit, meadow 65, 146, 155, 156
Psamma arenaria 145
Puffin 160

Razorbill 160
Redwing 129, 135, 137, 144, 160
Reid, Dr Archdall 82
Robin 64, 132, 136, 161, 163,
        164
Rolfe, John 166

Saffron cake 75
Samphire 48
Sandhills 137, 145
Scawen, William 115, 120
Seal 152, 153, 154, 156
Seine 55
Shag 48, 157
Shearwater 160
Silchester 34
Smith, Baker Peter 39, 40
Sparrow 15, 61, 62, 83, 87, 151,
        162
St. Ives 5, 7, 9, 10, 12, 13, 14, 15,
        16, 19, 22, 25, 33, 37, 48,
        51, 56, 64, 68, 105, 109,
        128, 129, 130, 131, 132,
        133, 137, 145, 146, 152,
        156, 166, 181
St. Michael's Mount 25
St. Sennen 188
Starling 61
Swinburne 178

Tamar, River 7, 31, 43, 97
Tennyson 92
Thrush 61, 144
Tol-Pedn-Penwith 38, 150
Tonkin 70
Towans (sandhills) 13, 145, 146
Towednack 100
Tregellas, J. T. 104
Treryn (Treen) Dinas 38
A Trip to the Far West 39

*An Unsentimental Journey through
        Cornwall* 184

Wagtail 61, 65, 136
Wells-by-the-Sea 155
Wesley brothers 40, 42, 85, 93,
        121, 122, 130, 131
Wheatear 10, 48, 181
White, Kirke 169
Whitesand Bay 118
Winter heliotrope 165, 169
Wolf lighthouse 41
Wren, Cornish 63

Zennor, cliffs 38, 101, 136, 138,
        141